Working with

DEMENTIA

Dedication

For my children, Liam and Rebecca, as they embark upon their journey through life. GS

To my parents, Ruby & John Goudie. FG

Working with

DEMENTIA

GRAHAM STOKES
FIONA GOUDIE

WINSLOW

Telford Road • Bicester
Oxon OX6 0TS • UK

WORKING WITH DEMENTIA

First published in 1990 by
Winslow Press Limited, Telford Road, Bicester, Oxon OX6 OTS, United Kingdom
Reprinted 1991, 1992, 1993, 1994, 1995, 1996

Phototypeset by Gecko Limited, Bicester, Oxon

02-856/Printed in Great Britain (HtP)

British Library Cataloguing in Publication Data
Stokes, Graham
    Working with dementia
    1. Dementia patients. Care
    I. Title   II. Goudie, Fiona
    362.2

ISBN 0–86388–084–3

CONTENTS

CONTRIBUTORS

Drew Alcott   Currently works as a senior clinical psychologist in Coventry on a multidisciplinary team which supports elderly mentally infirm and ill people in the community, and at the Neurosciences Unit, Walsgrave Hospital. He has been involved in training many people who work with the elderly in the social and health services around the country.

Beth Allen   Sister in charge of the Psychogeriatric Day Assessment Unit at Gulson Hospital, Coventry. She is interested in morale and stress among professionals working with dementing people.

Rosemary Bennett   An occupational therapist with North Warwickshire Social Services. She is interested in multidisciplinary assessment involving home helps and district nurses. She is also interested in bereavement and is a CRUSE counsellor.

Theresa Briscoe   A psychiatric nurse who has been involved in organising activity services for dementia sufferers in hospitals. She set up the Royal College of Nursing's *Activities Nurses* group.

Pam Enderby   District speech therapist with Frenchay Health Authority in Bristol.

Fiona Goudie   Principal clinical psychologist with Coventry Health Authority, she is experienced in the assessment and management of dementia in both institutional and community settings. In addition, she is the training officer for a voluntary agency which supports the families of confused elderly people. She is particularly interested in psychotherapy with older adults.

Una Holden   A principal clinical psychologist, Una is an established authority on RO therapy and the assessment of dementia. Her academic texts and practical handbooks include *RO Reminders*, *Looking at Confusion* and *Thinking it Through* (Winslow Press). She is a Fellow of the British Psychological Society.

Anita Steed   Head occupational therapist at John Connolly Hospital, Birmingham. She is actively involved in a community-based service for older adults.

Graham Stokes   A consultant clinical psychologist responsible for psychology services for elderly people in Coventry. He is an expert in the area of disruptive behaviour in dementia and is the author of the *Managing Common Problems* series published by Winslow Press.

John Wattis   A consultant psychogeriatrician and senior lecturer in old age psychiatry at St James's University Hospital, Leeds. He has conducted research into the development of psychiatric services for elderly people in the United Kingdom, into medical students' attitudes to elderly people, into alcohol abuse in old age and has co-authored a basic text, *Practical Psychiatry of Old Age*.

PREFACE

Working with Dementia starts from the viewpoint that staff caring for people suffering from dementia should be recognised as professionals who require or possess a specialist body of knowledge and skills.

Written in practical terms, this book promotes a client-centred approach to assessment and intervention. While it focuses upon practical skills, it also outlines the theoretical basis of these, and treats seriously the complexity which surrounds the very term *dementia*.

Born of our training experiences over the past five years, the structure of *Working with Dementia* has been thoughtfully considered to ensure that the content follows a logical progression from the meaning of normal and abnormal aging, to diagnosis and assessment, and on to issues of management and therapy. The text is divided into six sections:

1   *Setting the Scene* (Chapters 1 to 4)
This section examines attitudes to aging and dementia; what is to be expected in 'normal' aging in terms of memory and intellect, personality, adjustment and sexuality; and the causes and clinical picture of dementia and other mental health problems of late life.

2   *Discovery* (Chapters 5 to 9)
This section looks at the issues of client assessment, behaviour analysis and environmental design in order to gain a full understanding of dementia, and addresses the questions: What to assess; How to assess; and Why assess?

3   *Relearning & Rehabilitation* (Chapters 10 to 16)
Setting realistic and positive goals in order to promote independence and life quality through the provision of occupation and therapeutic activity are the concerns of this section. The theory and innovative practice of goal planning, reality orientation and reminiscence therapy are described alongside practical suggestions to encourage communication and promote the maintenance of lifelong interests and activities.

4   *Common Management Problems* (Chapters 17 to 19)
The presence of challenging, disruptive behaviours is often the reason for breakdown in family support and a source of strain for professional workers. This section dispels many unhelpful myths which surround behaviours like aggression, wandering and toileting difficulties by interpreting them as an

individual reaction to circumstances, rather than solely as a function of either brain disease or personality. A problem-solving approach is central to the development of programmes of prevention and management.

5   *Emotions* (Chapters 20 to 22)
The feelings of dementing people are often neglected, and carers sometimes ignore the fact that 'difficult' behaviour may be the consequence of the confused person being unable to express emotion and need. How can we help dementia sufferers negotiate the traumas they are experiencing? This section looks at the reasons for emotional problems, the role of medication and the effectiveness of counselling techniques such as resolution therapy and validation therapy.

6   *The Supporters* (Chapters 23 & 24)
Quality care is inextricably linked to the welfare and well-being of the support network. This section looks at the skills and resources which can help families who care for dementing relatives, and examines the needs of professional care-givers. If staff are valued and rewarded, they will be more able to work towards meeting the needs of their clients and patients.

This book can be read in its entirety, but the chapters are also written to stand alone, so that the reader can select topics which are relevant to current interest and concern.

Working with Dementia aims to contribute to the continuing development of ideas in what has in the past been an ignored area of clinical activity. For too long dementia remained a 'silent epidemic', devastating the lives of misunderstood victims and forgotten supporters.

We owe a debt of gratitude to all those people who have participated in our many training courses over recent years. They have continually sparked our enthusiasm and provided us with fresh and thought-provoking material. We hope that this book will help to satisfy the demand from professionals for greater knowledge about dementia and a wish for the horizons of care to be expanded through the application of creative thought to accepted theory and practice.

GRAHAM STOKES
FIONA GOUDIE
July 1990

PART 1

Setting the Scene

CHAPTER 1 *Fiona Goudie*

Attitudes to Aging & Dementia

The average life expectancy in the United Kingdom at birth now exceeds 70 years. By the turn of the century nearly nine million people will be aged 65 years or more. Nearly half of these will be over 75 and more than a million will be at least 85 years old (Office of Population, Census and Statistics, 1985). However diversity of life-style and expansion of interests are not seen as characteristic of this period and people of all ages may view life beyond 60 or 65 with reservations.

The ancient Romans saw old age as a disease and searched for a 'cure' which would lead to eternal life. More contemporarily, a group of 3–11-year-olds in one piece of research described older people as 'wrinkled, short and grey haired', who 'do not go out much, have heart attacks and die'. They stated that they did not want to grow old. People over 70 often classify themselves as middle-aged, which reinforces the stereotype that being old is an undesirable experience.

However aging cannot be defined in a single way. It can be viewed from different perspectives. Many changes take place as people grow older, so aging cannot simply be defined in terms of chronological age. Aging has a psychological perspective. This concerns the way individuals view themselves. Some see themselves as old or geriatric while others do not feel any older than when they were thirty or forty years of age. They may experience their advancing age as depressing or worrying, but also as positive and hopeful.

Aging is also socially prescribed. Society has arbitrary marks to distinguish old from young, such as an age for retirement and 'OAP' status. It also identifies family roles (grandparenthood) and has certain views about what behaviour is expected or accepted (as expressed, for example, by the accusation that a woman looks like 'mutton dressed as lamb'). Why is it that we often think that older people have less to offer than younger people, and is this why so many people view growing older with such trepidation?

Attitudes to Aging

Attitudes can be defined as the way in which we feel, think and behave towards something or someone. They are affected by the behaviour and opinions of those we come into contact with on a regular basis, as well as by our own experiences.

What is it that makes us think negatively about older people? Factors likely to influence us will include:

- The use of words relating to old age as insults (such as: crumblies, wrinklies, being senile, going demented);
- Factors such as life expectancy in the culture in which we live: the association of aging with death means that we are likely to view old age with concern;
- The lack of a high profile of healthy, active elderly people in public life, on television or in newspapers;
- Policy documents which suggest that there will be more older people than we will be able to care for as a society;
- Our own fears of age and infirmity in a society that emphasises the value of youth and beauty.

These sorts of factors are likely to have an impact on the way we think and feel about older people, so that we end up feeling it is better to be young than old. Many retired people reject terms like 'old age pensioner' as insulting and undignified. We may feel that we would prefer to be thirty or forty than seventy, but does this really mean that such attitudes can lead to older people being treated as second-class citizens?

The Effect of Attitudes on Behaviour

Examining the attitudes of professional groups towards older people in general suggests that attitudes do indeed affect the way we behave. Working with older people is seen as unattractive by trainee nurses, doctors, social workers, psychologists, occupational therapists and other professionals. The high number of job vacancies in these disciplines for staff to work with elderly people would seem to reflect this lack of appeal.

The lack of enthusiastic professionals working with older adults does mean that good training placements and high-quality teaching is limited. Even interested students may have to make considerable efforts to develop their skills and knowledge in this area. Training courses which do not devote time to the successes which can be achieved by those working with older adults who have problems may increase negative attitudes among students. Nursing and medical students seem to become more negative in their attitudes to older people as their training progresses (Gale and Livesley, 1974).

Qualified staff often think that work with older people does not require special skills. Social workers interviewed about their attitudes to older people felt that work with this client group was an unskilled task that required the arrangement of home help and meals on wheels, which could be dealt with by social work assistants rather than qualified staff (Nicholson and Paley, 1981).

Complaints about GPs made by older people also suggest that negative thinking about the abilities and capacities of their older patients might influence the treatment offered. Complaints made to groups such as the Patients' Association include:

'Automatically putting ill health down to old age';
'Being reluctant to refer older people for hospital investigations';
'Overwillingness to sedate';
'Failure to recognise dementia and depression' (Norman, 1986).

This prejudice against the need for active intervention or treatment for older people applies across professional groups. Reasons often given for lack of active treatment include beliefs that symptoms are irreversible and linked to aging, and feelings that elderly people will not attend for treatment or are resistant to change. Sometimes it is thought that older people have fewer years left to live, so extensive and expensive treatment will not be worthwhile.

Information from elderly people themselves contradicts these views. One of the most significant factors in non-attendance for hospital appointments or at day centres is poorly organised or non-existent transport. As far as irreversibility of symptoms or resistance to change are concerned, most older people adapt successfully to life after retirement, the death of a lifelong partner or physical frailty. Older adults with major problems which they are unable to cope with are in the minority.

Apart from lack of specialist training in how to help with problems in later life, there is often a lack of information on how 'normal' elderly people function. This is partly due to the lack of positive images of older people in the public domain, but also to the fact that those of us who work with older adults have no direct experience of what life is like for them. Often our professional knowledge is restricted to information about and observation of those with problems. The extensive contact with people who have mental health problems can mean that their experiences are taken to represent the life experience of most elderly people. Cognitive deterioration and dependency on others can come to be viewed as the norm. Rarely are healthy elderly people invited to evaluate courses, or services designed to meet the needs of those with an illness.

Attitudes and Dementia

It is true that the majority of those working with dementia sufferers care a great deal about their clients or patients. Yet, at times, because of the extreme dependency of the most severely impaired individuals, carers can end up treating them as if they have no meaningful life history. Indeed direct care staff without access to case notes, hospital records or discussions with relatives may not even know details of the person's previous occupation or family life. Sadly there are still carers who make comments like: "You need to talk to them like children", or "It is like looking after babies really, isn't it?"

It seems as if extensive contact with more cognitively impaired older adults distances people from awareness of what life is like for the majority and what life was like for their clients and patients before the onset of their illness. Treating adults as 'babies' is not only humiliating and inappropriate but it denies the possibility that individuals may retain certain abilities. People can become de-skilled if their needs are automatically met by others.

One of the most fundamental human rights is to be treated with dignity and respect as human beings. Of course this means that the dignity and respect has to be appropriate to our age and experience of life. Providing a level of care more suited to children or babies may meet physical needs, but not emotional ones.

Promoting Positive Staff Attitudes

Negative staff attitudes are frequently seen as the main barrier to improving the quality of care received by clients or patients in hospital and residential settings. Training is often proposed as a means by which staff can be encouraged to develop their knowledge and thus acquire more 'positive' attitudes. Attitudes are a function of upbringing and experience and cannot be easily changed by a teaching session; none the less, training to develop skills is important, as staff need to know how to put good ideas into practice.

What is most crucial is that the people selected to work with older adults are chosen on the basis of their respect for and wish to work with older people and not just on professional qualifications. The same should apply to unqualified care staff. It is easier to build good practices in care with a group of people who are enthusiastic about the people they work with, than to attempt to change the attitudes of people who would prefer to work with younger adults or in jobs unrelated to the field of caring.

Promoting positive attitudes in staff will be further enhanced if the work they do is seen as having status and requiring special skills. Work with elderly people with mental health problems requires skills other than those which would be required to work with healthy older adults. There is a need for training courses for those working with dementia sufferers and a recognised career development before staff begin to value themselves as specialists. Ease of entry into work in residential homes, particularly in the private sector, implies that special skills or qualities are not required.

In social and health service settings there may be opportunities for enthusiastic staff working with older people to undertake more advanced training in nursing or social work, with the associated possibilities of career enhancement. This needs to be maintained and developed in all areas concerned with the provision of care for older people.

Introduction of key worker systems into residential and home care programmes enables staff to view their work as client-orientated rather than task-orientated. (*See Chapter 10 for more on this.*) It seems that the more involved staff feel in the decisions being made about the care of their patients and clients, the more positive their attitudes are likely to be towards them.

Because of the lack of experience of aging amongst most people formulating policy, devising training and running services for older people there is a need for older adults to be involved in the evaluating and monitoring of services. Although patients' associations, consumers' groups and community health councils exist, they seldom have many older adults represented. One resident in an elderly person's home was keen to attend a course on 'Care of the Elderly' aimed at care staff. Although she had the support of the residents' group and a number of the staff, others saw her wish to be involved as nosiness.

Contact with healthy older people and an awareness of the normal physical and psychological changes likely to occur should be a part of basic training courses for all those intending to work with physically and mentally frail older adults (*see Chapter 2*). This allows staff to develop a sense of perspective about the abilities of their clients.

Experiential exercises involving 'instant aging' are popular with trainers. These involve trainees wearing blindfolds or earplugs or spending half a day in a wheelchair to understand the experience of and empathise with those with sensory and physical losses. Age awareness exercises (see Itzin, 1986, for a fuller discussion) involve examining how we acquired our own prejudices, re-evaluating these prejudices and deciding to behave in different ways in our work settings. Participants in the exercises need to agree to respect confidentiality, not to ridicule or criticise others for their feelings and to avoid defensiveness. Group leaders in these types of exercises must be experienced in dealing with the powerful feelings that may develop. This type of exercise rarely works when all participants are from one work setting, as people feel their honesty may be used against them in their jobs. Also such training sessions need time, perhaps one or two days, to give everyone a chance to speak and listen. Trying to include age awareness as a one- or two-hour slot in a training course on aging will not work. People need time to get beyond the usual 'age is relative' response which many professionals give when asked questions such as 'What is old age?'

Conclusion

This chapter has explored some of the reasons for the existence of negative attitudes towards growing older. It has discussed the problems with which negative attitudes may be associated in caring for elderly people with dementia. Although it is acknowledged that changing attitudes is not an easy process, some suggestions have been made in terms of staff recruitment, training and service delivery which aim to minimise the effects of negative attitudes.

Alison Norman (1986) concludes that:

"... the most powerful weapon of all in the fight against ageism is to remember that the average expectation of life at birth is now more than 70 years. Failing a nuclear holocaust, almost all of us will live to be old, and many of us will be very old. It is in our own interest to combat ageism ..."

Perhaps now is the time to think about the attitudes we would like to develop and pass on to ensure that every older person who requires care is treated exactly as we would wish to be treated ourselves.

REFERENCES

Gale J and Livesley B 'Attitudes Towards Geriatrics: A Report of the Kings Survey', *Age and Aging*, 3, pp 49–53, 1974.

Itzin C 'Ageism Awareness Training: A Model for Group Work', in C Phillipson, M Bernard and P Strang (eds) *Dependency and Interdependency in Old Age: Theoretical Perspectives and Policy Alternatives*, Croom Helm, Beckenham, Kent (in association with the British Society of Gerontology) 1986.

Nicholson N and Paly J 'What are the Principles of Practice?', *Community Care*, 30 July 1981.

Norman A *Aspects of Ageism: A Discussion Paper*, Centre for Policy on Ageing, London, 1986.

Office of Population, Census and Statistics *Social Trends*, 15, 1985.

Normal Aging

Why have a chapter on normal aging in a book about dementia? Those working with elderly people are often called upon to distinguish normal from abnormal and are involved in 'normalising' services for those with dementia. To do this an understanding of normal aging is important.

Aging

Although we can distinguish different aspects of aging (biological, social and psychological) there is a great deal of overlap and interaction between them. Physical change such as arthritis can limit mobility, which in turn can reduce involvement in social activities or other previous sources of enjoyment. The isolation can produce a sense of loneliness, helplessness and even depression. In this state memory and concentration may be affected. The fact that one facet of aging can influence another must be remembered when considering changes in cognitive functions.

Definition of normal

Many people misunderstand the idea of normality. They tend to think of normal and abnormal as being opposite poles. In fact 'normality' refers to the range around the middle of a dimension (eg. height) with two extremes at opposite ends (very tall and very short), rather than one extreme. The very middle of a dimension is the average, on either side of which is the range of normality. This range can be wide or narrow, but all those who fall within it are classed as normal. What at first impression may be thought to be abnormal may often in fact be within the normal range.

It is also important to remember that, often, people have their own opinion about what is normal and abnormal, but this may have little basis in reality. Their picture of what is normal for elderly people may be based on a false stereotype. A problem is that what is seen as normal is more likely to be seen as acceptable. This can lead to the maintenance of myths. For example, years ago it was considered normal for a person to suffer poor health and death in their 60s. Had this been passively accepted we would not have seen the changes in health care and life expectancy which we accept as normal today.

It is important not to be complacent in setting standards when dealing with elderly people. We should remember that we are all going to get old and so we need to ask ourselves whether what we feel is normal and acceptable for elderly people today would be acceptable to us.

Cognitive Changes Associated with Aging

When we refer to cognitive functions we are referring to the higher mental functions of the brain. The brain is involved in many basic functions, such as controlling body temperature, breathing and heart rate, and enabling activities such as walking. Cognitive functions include mental abilities such as memory, concentration, language and planning future actions.

The brain is an organ and it changes physically with age. There is a gradual reduction in the number of brain cells and the amount of blood flow to the brain becomes reduced. There are also changes in the properties of the brain cells which can influence their functioning. This no doubt underlies some of the cognitive changes associated with aging; however such physical alterations often occur without any noticeable cognitive changes. There is rarely any apparent reduction in an elderly person's ability to cope with daily activities of living.

Sensory factors

Without information from the senses the brain could not function. A reduction in the quality of sensory input because of deafness or poor eyesight places extra demands on the higher cognitive functions. Older adults with sensory deficits have been found to show some impairment in cognitive tests. This can be similar in appearance to impairments found in dementia, but is not the same because it can be improved with sensory aids. This shows that cognitive abilities do not depend only upon how efficiently the brain is working.

Intelligence and complex problem-solving

It was once thought that intelligence declined gradually with age from mid-life onwards. This belief was based on cross-sectional studies which used intelligence tests to compare people in their 20s and 30s with those in their 60s and 70s.

The problem with cross-sectional studies is that they tend to overlook differences in the experiences of each age group. The childhood experiences of older generations are different from those of younger generations. In particular, the education of people brought up 40 and 60 years ago was different. This is important because most intelligence tests are affected by the nature and degree of a person's education.

Longitudinal studies help to overcome this problem by comparing the person's performance after a period of time has passed. If they are different at the age of 60 from what they were at 40 this is more likely to represent a change due to aging (although other things which happened to them over that time need to be considered too).

Longitudinal studies do show that there is a decline in intelligence, but this does not happen until after so-called 'old-old' age. That is, above the age of seventy-five. This change is not inevitable, since it is not found in everyone over seventy-five. Maintaining a high performance level in intelligence tests is associated with a number of factors. These include higher education, relatively high income during working life, with reasonable savings, good physical health and mobility, and maintaining leisure and social activities.

Different aspects of intelligence have been described and these are differently affected by aging. *Crystalline intelligence* involves the use of stored knowledge and information to answer questions or solve problems previously encountered. This ability changes little with age, and is akin to wisdom. *Fluid intelligence* is more flexible and adaptable, is characterised by the ability to reason and to abstract and is involved in solving problems not previously encountered. This area of ability has been found to decline in older adults.

Such changes as are found in the laboratory are not necessarily noticeable in real-life activities, except under quite demanding conditions which require fluid intelligence. A noticeable reduction in problem solving ability is more likely above the age of seventy but is less likely to be seen in people of high intelligence.

Memory and learning

Deterioration of memory is one of the hallmarks of dementia. Even among normal older people poorer memory is often expected and accepted as part of getting old. People report difficulty in remembering names, faces, or where they have put things, but they say they can remember things from the past without difficulty.

Memory is not a single process but comprises several aspects. Information is taken in (ie learned), stored and used (ie recalled) at a later time. Some information is held for only a brief time in 'primary' memory, while some is stored more permanently in 'secondary' memory. Secondary memory is relevant to day-to-day living. It has been suggested that remote or long-term memory is a separate process, enabling people to reminisce about past events.

Changes in learning and memory abilities have been found in older people. Although they are still able to learn as much as younger people, they need more time to achieve the same level of learning. In other words they cannot take in information as quickly. This probably has to do with the speed of information processing discussed below.

Learning and memory are interlinked, so it is not surprising that some decline in primary and secondary memory is found in older adults, although changes are relatively small. It is not true, however, that remote memory is spared. Although it is more difficult to test remote memory, there is evidence that recall of distant memories is also affected with advancing age.

Speed of information/mental processes

One simple but reliable measure of how well the brain functions is the speed at which it can work. Basically the faster it can work (ie process information) the better it is able to work. With increasing age there is a definite slowing of the speed at which the nervous system functions. This affects not only motor (eg. manual) speed but also the speed of information processing. This is important because other cognitive functions such as learning and memory will suffer as a result of such slowing.

Language

Changes in language abilities are another common characteristic of dementia, but, as there are also less severe changes found in normal older people, such changes are not necessarily indicative of dementia. About 15 per cent of normal older adults produce errors such as those found in dementia.

People's voice characteristics tend to change with age. From the fifth decade pitch becomes higher, resonance thinner, and volume is lower. Various factors, such as smoking, stooped posture, unclean environment (eg. dust) or prolonged abuse of the voice can contribute to this. From the sixth decade speech may become slower and less clearly articulated. This may be due to toothlessness or ill-fitting dentures or weakening of the muscles involved in speech production.

Powers of comprehension may decline, owing to various factors, such as poor hearing, reduced primary memory capacity and difficulty with handling competing stimuli. Hearing impairments are particularly important since they occur in about 40 per cent of those older than 75 and are known to compromise cognitive functions generally. By the seventh decade people show more difficulty understanding the subtle messages of inference, ambiguity and anomaly. However the ability to use semantic information (ie the meaning of words) remains stable.

Personality

The stereotype of the personality in old age is of the person becoming more self-centred, garrulous, hypochondriacal and withdrawn. Personality changes occur in dementia but it is difficult to differentiate between cognitive change and alterations in personality.

The studies of personality change with age also suffer from the problem mentioned above with regard to studies of intelligence. They too are often based on cross-sectional methods. We do know, however, that, contrary to the stereotype, major personality changes do not normally take place: with advancing age the personality remains relatively stable. If any change does occur, the person may become slightly more introverted and socially withdrawn. A major question is whether this is by choice or by force of circumstances, such as decreased mobility, limited finances and reduction of their social network.

One suggestion is that people strive to achieve and maintain continuity and consistency throughout their lifetime. Rather than changing, it could be said that people become even more emphatically themselves with age as personality traits become more pronounced.

Social Adaptation

The majority of older people adjust to events in late life. A small proportion are extremely well adjusted, while about 30 per cent experience some problems of adjustment. Studies suggest that these are individuals who are at odds with themselves, others around them, and their environment.

To understand what contributes to good adjustment we must look to the interplay between the person and their environment. Because aging involves various losses (for example, death of partner, impaired health, loss of occupation and status), the environment usually presents numerous adverse events to which the person must adjust.

However the environment can also have beneficial aspects, such as a supportive social network. Family support often remains strong. In social and family relationships it is the quality of the relationships which is most important. One or two close, confiding relationships are more valuable than many acquaintances. The individual's own coping resources are also important. There is evidence that older people may be better able to cope and adjust to stresses such as bereavement.

Sexuality

Whilst the general expectation that older people will not be sexually active is a major factor in reducing sexual activity among elderly people, there is, in fact, a great deal of variation in sexual interest and activity. What often appears to be the most important influence on sexuality in elderly women is the availability of a capable partner. In men sexual function can continue into extreme old age, with past sexual interest, frequency and enjoyment as the best predictors of function in late life. Overall, given good health and appropriate circumstances, sexual activity can be a rewarding feature of old age.

Conclusion

It is clear that some deterioration of cognitive functions is associated with normal aging. This is not due to any disease or abnormal brain damage but to age-related changes in the brain. Although some of these changes (eg. slower speed of processing) may begin in mid-life, most do not appear until later old age. However, it is not the case that everyone will inevitably show signs of deterioration. Overall, it is unlikely that changes in cognitive functions will be significant enough to begin to affect the person's ability to function in daily activities. Those who are more likely to retain a high level of abilities are those who entered their older years already functioning above the normal. Social and economic factors will also play a protective role. Those who are in a position to maintain their health and an active physical and social life will fare better. Those who are handicapped by impaired vision or hearing have an added hindrance.

There is a group of elderly people who are exceptionally well preserved in physical and emotional health and who are free from social difficulties. They have a high level of involvement in activities both within and outside the home and survive for longer than would be expected. They have been referred to as 'super-normal'!

FURTHER READING

Birren J E and Sloane R B, *Handbook of Mental Health and Aging*, Prentice Hall, Englewood Cliffs, NJ, 1980.
Holden U, *Neuropsychology of Aging*, Croom Helm, London, 1988.
Woods R T and Britton P G, *Clinical Psychology with the Elderly*, Croom Helm, London, 1985.
Zarit S, *Aging and Mental Disorders*, Collier MacMillan, London, 1980.

CHAPTER 3

Graham Stokes & Una Holden

Dementia: Causes & Clinical Syndromes

*D*espite general belief, dementia is *not* a disease in its own right. It is, essentially, a set of signs and symptoms indicating a need for further investigations. To put it simply, if a person is showing major signs of intellectual or social deterioration the reason should be sought. As has been detailed in the previous chapter, such changes are not to be expected as part of 'normal' aging.

Dementia can be the result of many things and in some instances the condition may be reversible. As is shown later in the chapter, once these underlying diseases and disorders are diagnosed and treated the dementia responds and the person may return to 'normal'. However certain diseases cannot be treated and the patient is faced with a devastating illness which will destroy their true self long before the body dies. Such dementing illnesses are often termed '*primary dementias*' and it is these which are the principal subject of this book.

Primary dementia may be defined as an extensive, organic impairment of intellect, memory and personality in the absence of clouding of consciousness (ie without drowsiness) which is acquired, irreversible and progressive.

How Common is Dementia?

Among people aged over 65 the prevalence (ie the percentage of people afflicted at a given time) of moderate to severe dementia has been estimated at between 1.3 and 6.2 per cent. Such a wide range in prevalence rates is likely to be the result of different methods of identifying dementia. The median (ie the mid-point) prevalence rate suggests that about 4.5 per cent of the over-65s are afflicted with a dementing illness. This means that, in England today, around 365,000 elderly people are suffering from dementia.

There is a marked increase in prevalence with age: between the ages of 65 and 74 prevalence is approximately 2.5 per cent, yet for those people aged over 80 the rate may be as high as 22 per cent. This dramatic increase is a matter for concern, for the number of people in this age group will double by the end of the century, largely as a result of reduced mortality among those surviving into late life. There will therefore be many more people suffering from an irreversible dementia by the end of the decade than are found today. However it is possible that prevalence declines in those people aged 90 and over.

In addition to severe dementia, mild forms have been estimated as occurring in between 2.6 and 20.0 per cent of the elderly. Unfortunately, as such disparity makes clear, these figures are unreliable and difficult to interpret. In a proportion of cases the intellectual impairment identified will be the product of non-progressive or reversible organic disease, or emotional disorder. If stringent diagnostic criteria are not employed the prevalence of irreversible, progressive dementia can easily be overestimated. There are a number of reports where longitudinal studies of elderly people over several years have failed to identify progressive deterioration despite an earlier diagnosis of mild dementia.

The incidence rate (ie frequency of new cases occurring) appears to be approximately 1 per cent of the elderly population aged over 65.

Demographic Factors

There are more women than men suffering from dementia. The reasons for this are unclear. However, it is likely that the finding is in large part due to the increased life expectancy of women, coupled with the greater prevalence of dementia in the ninth decade of life.

The racial and ethnic distribution of dementia is currently unknown. There are no prevalence studies of dementia in Third-World countries. The relationship with social class appears uncertain. Little is known of the geographical variation in the prevalence of dementia, although there is no reason to assume that the rates of dementia are the same everywhere.

The Causes of Primary Dementia

Alzheimer's Disease (AD)

This is the most common form of dementia, accounting for approximately 50 per cent of classified cases. Definite AD cannot be diagnosed without autopsy, although a particular pattern of progressive generalised deterioration in the absence of other disease is usually sufficient to indicate its presence.

Onset may occur as early as the fifth decade of life. It follows an insidious, unremitting course over several years, from subtle impairment of memory and the higher mental abilities, such as judgement and abstract thinking in the early stages, to virtual disintegration of the intellect and personality and the development of a state of total dependency.

Following Alois Alzheimer's presentation, in 1906, of the disease in a middle-aged woman the syndrome was regarded as an exclusively pre-senile dementia. The distinction was made between Alzheimer's Disease and senile dementia, the latter having an onset at or after 65 years. Whilst the characteristic AD picture of intellectual and behavioural deterioration represented a dramatic and tragic deviation from normal aging, a diagnosis of senile dementia was often felt to be an inevitable consequence of late life. Knowledge was disfigured by myth and distorted by diagnostic inaccuracy. Psychiatric disorders, such as depression, and cognitive deterioration arising from poor physical health were considered alongside progressive brain disease as different manifestations of senile degeneration of the brain.

With the development of a greater understanding of intellectual functioning and behavioural performance in old age (*see Chapter 2*) and more accurate clinical diagnosis, ignorance is in retreat. It is now known that a picture of progressive impairment over a period of years, the onset and course of which is gradual, is, in the main, both clinically and neuropathologically indistinguishable from AD. However, as with other diseases, such as cancer, younger people are more rapidly and severely affected. Kinship with AD is now generally accepted, yet the idea of a dichotomy persists, so late-onset dementia is now referred to as Senile Dementia of the Alzheimer Type (SDAT).

Whilst the dichotomy between AD and SDAT is artificial and archaic, it is true to say that in late-onset dementia the Alzheimer-type neuropathologic changes (namely, senile plaques and neurofibrillary tangles) may differ in formation and distribution. Not only are the reasons for this unclear, it is also the case that many aged people who have no demonstrable cognitive impairment reveal the same pathological alterations as dementia sufferers. This latter finding can be explained if such changes are seen as a feature of aging. However for AD sufferers a 'critical' threshold level will have been exceeded. If pathological changes are numerous and located throughout the cerebral cortex, intellectual decline and behavioural deterioration will be profound and SDAT will be diagnosed. If they are few in number, 'normal' aging is preserved. Thus, in old age, development may be placed on a continuum from normal aging to SDAT. Benign Senescent Forgetfulness (BSF), an age-associated memory decline which does not indicate the onset of widespread intellectual devastation, can be seen as a point on the continuum between normal aging and dementia.

Risk factors

As a person ages, their position on the continuum could depend on exposure to a number of risk factors of which only a few have been identified so far. Apart from age, head injury, Down's syndrome and a family history of Down's syndrome have been implicated. Heredity appears to be of some importance, as close relatives of a sufferer do have a greater risk of developing AD. It would appear that the risk to relatives varies, depending on the age at which the disease began. There is a decrease in risk with late age onset.

Controversy surrounds the role of possible environmental toxins, such as aluminium. One study in England found the incidence of AD was related to the level of aluminium in the water supply. However the case remains not proven. Overall, AD remains a devastating disease of unknown cause.

The clinical syndrome

The course of cognitive, behavioural and emotional change varies from person to person. However, whilst there is no common pathway, a stage model which describes broad characteristics is generally accepted (eg. Riesberg, 1983).

The 'Forgetfulness Phase' (minimal–mild dementia). In this first stage the most prominent feature is short-term memory loss. There is difficulty in recalling recent events, and a tendency to forget where objects have been placed. Disorientation in time frequently occurs. Names of places and people which had once been familiar may also be poorly recalled. Fatigue and poor concentration may be observed. Abstract thinking shows signs of patchy impairment. The 'new' or unexpected will be feared or disliked. Sufferers lack curiosity and appear egotistical as they seek sanctuary in established routines. There may be emotional changes such as anxiety and irritability. Reactions to the distressing changes may result in additional psychopathology which may obscure the advancing cognitive decline. Denial may be used as a defence against the emotional trauma of losing one's intellectual capacity.

The 'Confusional Phase' (mild–moderate dementia). This stage is characterised by deteriorating memory, increasingly poor attention-span and a decline in generalised intellectual performance. Disorientation in place can result in the person getting lost in unfamiliar surroundings. The person may dwell on the past. Silly speech errors occur and a word-finding difficulty arises. Judgement and the capacity for abstract thought are significantly deteriorated. Although not inevitable, heightened confusion may result in disruptive behaviour such as wandering, aggression and unreasonable demands. Complex tasks are slovenly and inaccurately performed. The skills a person learned last will be lost first. So skills necessary for social independence and occupation will be the first to be markedly eroded. There is a withdrawal from challenging situations. Mood is characterised by emotional flattening. Rationalisations and confabulation (giving an imaginary account of activities and actions) are used to conceal failures of memory. Indifference towards family news and a loss of interest in events in general is to be expected.

The 'Dementia Phase' (moderate–severe dementia). This can be defined as beginning at the point at which remaining intellectual and self-care abilities would no longer sustain survival if the person was left on their own. Difficulties in basic activities of daily living are the hallmarks of this phase. Behaviour lacks purpose and appears disjointed. There is gross destruction of all intellectual capacities. Calculating ability is lost. Memory worsens to such an extent that personal history is eroded. As the stage progresses the ability to recognise oneself and close relatives is lost. All aspects of language are severely impoverished and ultimately lost. Insight disappears. Sufferers lose the urge or ability to practise intimate self-care skills and so need assistance in dressing, toileting and feeding.

The sufferer is unaware of their experiences and surroundings. The real person is now submerged by the disease. There is a progressive physical wasting as the person declines to a state of incoherent dependency. Ultimately physical feebleness will mean they require help in walking. Life may continue for one or more years in an almost vegetative state.

Progress through each of these stages is gradual. A person may spend several months, if not years, in each phase. It is important to note, however, that while remorseless deterioration is inevitable a surprising number of 'islands' of relatively intact ability will be found until late in the process. What functions are preserved and for how long will depend on the personal characteristics and history of the dementing person, as well as the encouragement received from care-givers.

Multi-infarct dementia (MID)

MID is a fluctuating and remitting vascular dementia characterised by an abrupt onset. It is generally observed in the seventh and eighth decades of life, although it may occur as early as the mid-forties. After AD, MID is the most common form of dementia, accounting for possibly as many as 20 per cent of cases. It is also important to recognise that the brains of AD sufferers are more vulnerable to vascular disease. Port-mortem studies have revealed that among patients with dementia 20 per cent had a mixture of AD and MID.

The course is typically that of a series of small strokes or 'strokelets' which vary in frequency, intensity and location from individual to individual. They cause episodes of confusion and loss of specific cognitive function, sometimes associated with minor neurological signs (for example, slurring of speech, weakness down one side of the body). In MID physical disability is not severe, unlike the case of a patient with a serious stroke. After the infarct there is usually limited clinical improvement until the next episode, which sometimes takes place in a matter of weeks or months, and sometimes not for more than a year. Eventually, however, after a succession of infarcts there is less and less recovery, until, by a process of 'step-wise' deterioration, dementia as profound as AD develops. However, many victims die before they reach the stage of advanced dementia, most often from a major stroke.

The clinical picture is patchy, inconsistent and at times intriguing. Certain intellectual functions are significantly deteriorated, while others are unimpaired. The characteristic indicators of MID can be seen in Table 3.1. Early

Table 3.1
Characteristic
indicators of MID

Process

1. An abrupt onset
2. Step-wise deterioration
3. A fluctuating course as improvement is seen after a cerebral infarct, followed by deterioration caused by the next one

Clinical Signs

1. Focal neurological signs, including aphasias, apraxias and agnosias (*see Chapter 4*)
2. Focal neurological symptoms, such as weakness of the face, arm or leg
3. Nocturnal confusion occurs most often in MID
4. Relative preservation of personality
5. Depression is more common in MID, partly because of the greater preservation of insight
6. Physical complaints can be a result of either depression or the discomfort in mobility and sensation caused by the cerebral infarcts
7. Emotional incontinence is sometimes very marked; weeping may be easily induced

Risk Factors

1. A history of hypertension
2. A history of strokes
3. Evidence of arteriosclerosis

recognition and treatment of the underlying disease (for example, hypertension, cardiac disease, arteriosclerosis) may arrest or inhibit further deterioration. Table 3.2 illustrates the differences between MID and AD.

Pick's Disease

This dementia begins most often between the ages of 45 and 60. Onset, progress and outcome are similar to those of Alzheimer's Disease. As a result, this rare disease is very difficult to differentiate from AD until the brain pathology is

Table 3.2
AD and MID:
differential
diagnosis

AD	**MID**
■Gradual deterioration	■Abrupt onset
■Progressive change	■Step-wise deterioration
■Widespread intellectual loss	■Focal neurological signs
■Docility and emotional blunting	■Emotionality
■No known health predictors	■Pre-morbid health indicators (eg. hypertension, stroke)
■Most common in women	■Most common in men

established after death. However it has been observed that early Pick's dementia is characterised by disinhibition, confabulation and fatuous emotion, while memory and intellect are relatively preserved. These more noticeable personality changes often overshadow any loss of intellectual ability. This is not the case in AD, where cognitive alterations are prominent early in the dementia.

Creuzfeldt-Jakob Disease (CJD)

CJD is an extremely rare pre-senile dementia, occurring in approximately one per million of the population. It usually begins in the fifth and sixth decades of life. The cause of CJD has been traced to the action of a slow-acting transmissible virus which produces a spongy change within the cerebral cortex.

The dementia progresses rapidly, duration being a matter of several months, rather than years. The first stage is characterised by fatigue, apathy, memory disturbance and disruptive behaviour. In the next phase, epilepsy, unsteady gait and emotional lability are present. Eventually a psychotic picture may develop.

Alcohol-related dementia

Prolonged alcohol abuse can lead in many cases to a progressive dementia similar to Alzheimer's Disease. There is an impairment of memory, a decline in general intellectual capacity, emotional instability and skill loss resulting in self-neglect. Delusions may also be present.

Alcohol-related dementia can be distinguished from another alcohol-induced problem, known as Korsakoff's disease, which also produces memory loss. This disease affects the person's memory for recent events, so that they have no recollection of what has happened moments earlier. The sufferer is disorientated in time and place, although the extent of memory loss is obscured by the person's ability to confabulate. This does not represent a conscious attempt to disguise the truth, for they have no awareness of their condition. However general intellectual performance is not affected, nor is there a progressive memory decline. If Korsakoff's disease is identified and treated early enough some remission is possible.

Subcortical dementia

While the syndrome of subcortical dementia was first described in 1912, it is only during the past decade that further progress has been made in our understanding of this condition. Whereas the dementias already described in this chapter are associated with diseases primarily involving the cerebral cortex (for example, AD), and are thus referred to as cortical dementias, in subcortical dementia the most notable pathological changes involve subcortical brain structures and mechanisms.

The clinical picture of subcortical dementia reflects the interruption of fundamental functions of motivation, arousal, timing and mood, resulting in exaggerated forgetfulness, slowing of thought and action, poor concentration, difficulties with problem-solving, and emotional disorder, particularly depression. Table 3.3 lists the contrasting features of cortical and subcortical dementia. Overall, gross deterioration in subcortical dementia is often apparent rather than real. The sadness and frustration of being dismissed as useless by those around can lead to an unwillingness to try and may thus give rise to a picture of profound deterioration.

The dementia associated with Parkinson's Disease (PD), Huntington's disease and progressive supranuclear palsy is typical of the subcortical pattern of cognitive impairment (Peretz and Cummings, 1988). Depending on the location of the 'strokelets', MID may be characterised by a mixed picture of cortical and subcortical dementia.

While the existence of cortical dementia is widely known and accepted, the relationship between subcortical disease and dementia is more controversial. The prevalence of subcortical dementia is in itself an area of controversy.

Characteristics	Subcortical dementia	Cortical dementia
Severity of the syndrome	Mild–moderate throughout most of the course	Severe deficits arise earlier in the profile of deterioration
Memory	Recall aided by clues and the passage of time	Not helped by clues
Language	Predominantly normal, but possibility of mild naming problems, dysarthria and mutism	Marked impairment of both expression and understanding
Personality	Apathy and irritability	Indifference, occasional disinhibition
Depression	Common	Uncommon
Movement	Slow	Normal, until late in the disease
Cause	For example, Parkinson's Disease, Huntington's Disease	For example, Alzheimer's Disease, Pick's Disease

Table 3.3
The contrasting clinical features of subcortical and cortical dementia

Current feeling is that earlier reports overestimate its occurrence. Research has also suggested that many PD patients have a higher incidence of brain alterations characteristic of AD than normal. This, it is felt, may cause or accentuate the dementia found in some, although clearly not in all cases of PD. The clinical syndrome which develops does not differ in quality from AD. Some investigators (for example, Knight *et al.*, 1988) believe there is no evidence from studies with PD patients to show that what has been termed subcortical dementia is anything other than the early stages of AD dementia.

The uncertainty regarding the extent and nature of the dementia associated with subcortical diseases such as PD is clearly a diagnostic issue which has yet to be resolved, although the existence of a subcortical variant appears increasingly probable.

Reversible or Treatable Dementias

If the condition causing the dementia is treatable, so is the dementia; in other words the process of deterioration can be reversed or at least arrested. Examples of these 'secondary' dementias are:

Chronic Subdural Haemotoma: Head injury may not give rise to symptoms of a progressive dementia until weeks or months after the incident. Headaches and drowsiness are usual. There is often a striking fluctuation in severity of the symptoms from day to day. Without surgical treatment death is the likely outcome.

Space-Occupying Lesions: Dementia is particularly associated with slowly growing brain tumours, especially meningiomas involving the frontal lobes. Cerebral tumour must be considered when investigations suggest an abnormality on one side of the brain only.

Normal Pressure Hydrocephalus: This condition is commonly diagnosed in the sixth and seventh decades of life, but may occur at any age. The build-up of cerebrospinal fluid pressure results in a progressive memory impairment. This may show some fluctuation from time to time. Unsteadiness of gait (ie ataxia) is common. Urinary incontinence is frequent. There may be a history of meningitis, head injury or neurosurgical operations. The introduction of a 'shunt' often produces a dramatic improvement. However if surgical intervention is long-delayed then deterioration is likely to be arrested rather than reversed.

Syphilis: Neurosyphilitic dementia used to account for 5 per cent of admissions to psychiatric hospitals at the beginning of this century. It is now rare because syphilis can be successfully treated at all stages by large doses of penicillin. Signs of dementia may not show until 20 years after the original infection.

Vitamin Deficiencies: Vitamin B12 deficiency can produce a fluctuating picture of dementia.

Endocrine Disturbances: Hypothyroidism occurs most commonly between the ages of 40 and 60 years and is more frequently observed in women. Intellectual deterioration arises early. Depression or paranoia may be prominent. If appropriate treatment does not occur until two years or more after the onset of cognitive loss there is an appreciable risk that recovery will be only partial.

Chronic Traumatic Encephalopathy: Repeated head injury such as boxers experience can result in this condition, otherwise known as 'dementia pugilistica'. Emotional and personality changes are early signs, soon accompanied by progressive cognitive decline. A Parkinsonian picture is common (*see Chapter 5 for a description of Parkinson's Disease*). Slow progression occurs but this may be arrested at any stage. A symptom-free period of five to ten years may intervene between retirement from boxing and the onset of dementia.

Conclusion

These many examples of dementia, with their differing underlying pathologies and prognoses, require a period of rigorous assessment. All possible explanations need to be considered and investigated when dementia is first seen. The fact that the person may be in their 70s and 80s does not preclude a treatable condition and thus they should not be prejudiced against solely on the basis of their age. Whilst investigations previously had their dangers for older people, in the present era techniques are straightforward and unthreatening.

The future holds the prospect that in all probability the incidence of irreversible dementia will drop as research continues to identify as yet undiscovered causes responsive to medical intervention.

REFERENCES

Knight R G, Godfrey H P D and Shelton E J, 'The Psychological Deficits Associated with Parkinson's Disease', *Clinical Psychology Review* 8, pp 391–410, 1988.

Peretz J A and Cummings J L, 'Subcortical Dementia', in U Holden (ed.) *Neuropsychology and Aging*, Croom Helm, London, 1988.

Riesberg B, 'An overview of current concepts of Alzheimer's Disease, Senile Dementia, and Age-Associated Cognitive Decline', in B Riesberg (ed.) *Alzheimer's Disease, the Standard Reference*', The Free Press, New York, 1983.

FURTHER READING

Jorm A F, *Understanding Senile Dementia*, Croom Helm, London, 1987.

Problems of Aging

There are many causes of confusion which are not due to a dementing process and which may be treatable. Often, however, these conditions are not recognised for what they are and can be wrongly labelled. This chapter examines some of these conditions, looks at how they can be identified and considers some of the treatment and interventions used to help people with them.

Physical Problems

Acute confusional state

This is very commonly confused with a dementing process. In fact an acute confusional state is not a condition but a consequence of change in the body's metabolism which leads to high temperature, fever and delirium, which in turn can cause temporary disorientation, memory loss, a state of 'muddled perplexity', poor concentration, hallucinations, clouding of consciousness and restlessness.

Such metabolic change can be due to many factors, ranging from illness to environmental changes and loss, some of which are shown in Table 4.1. Usually an acute state of confusion arises suddenly over a few days and as a result a person's behaviour is markedly different from normal. Unlike the situation where the person is suffering from dementia, the disorientation and confusion will improve if the underlying cause is treated. Regular physical check-ups play a valuable role here in ensuring that health problems and reactions to medication are dealt with before they lead to anything serious. Misdiagnosis does occur and is particularly common if a person is over 65 years old.

Table 4.1
Causes of acute
confusional state

- Toxicity due to: excessive medication, taking medication prescribed for someone else, side-effects of some drugs or reaction to a combination of drugs
- Poor diet, reduced fluid intake, excess alcohol consumption
- Endocrine disturbances such as diabetes or thyrotoxicosis
- Cerebral hypoxia caused by anaemia, pneumonia and transient ischaemic attacks
- Chest and urinary tract infections
- Renal failure
- Heart disease
- Trauma following a fracture or surgery
- Hypothermia
- Faecal impaction
- Sensory deprivation due to poor sight, poor hearing and social isolation
- Night-time or early morning wakening, which leads to excess fatigue
- Environmental changes such as moving house or going into hospital or residential care
- Grief reaction to bereavement, loss of home or loss of physical health

Case study 1

Mrs Raymond had recently moved to live in a sheltered flat. On arrival she seemed cheerful and capable of cooking simple snacks and carrying out light household tasks. She suffered from arthritis, so she had a daily home help to deal with shopping and other chores. She could not get outside the flat complex because of poor mobility, but enjoyed the regular coffee mornings and bingo sessions in the communal lounge. The flat's warden noticed, over a four- or five-day period, that Mrs Raymond had become listless, unkempt and socially withdrawn. She did not seem to know where she was and did not recognise the warden, with whom she was previously on first name terms. The warden noticed that Mrs Raymond rarely moved from her armchair and had been incontinent twice.

Talking Point: What do you think might be wrong here?

Mrs Raymond's GP was called, he examined her and she was admitted to the local hospital with a severe chest infection. This was treated with the appropriate medication and in two weeks Mrs Raymond was back home. She was thinner and a little more frail physically, but keen to build up her strength and resume her social life. The apathy, disorientation and incontinence had disappeared completely.

Parkinson's Disease

This neurological condition affects the basal ganglia, an area in the subcortical area of the brain which is responsible for co-ordinating motor action. Symptoms include tremor, rigidity, slowness of movement and postural problems. The most common form is idiopathic (unexplained) Parkinson's Disease which arises in one or two people in every thousand. Two-thirds of people with Parkinson's Disease show the first sign of symptoms between the ages of 50 and 69. The condition can also arise as a side-effect of some forms of medication, particularly neuroleptic drugs used for the treatment of psychotic illnesses like schizophrenia.

In the later stages of the illness, a proportion of patients will also be suffering from dementia. Some researchers consider that this type of dementia is consistent with the presentation of Alzheimer's Disease (Knight *et al*, 1988) while others believe that it is primarily a subcortical dementia (Cummings, 1986). Chapter 3 discusses the dementias in more detail. In the early stages of Parkinson's Disease cognitive functioning is usually intact, but, because of the severe motor difficulties which occur and the fact that about two-fifths of Parkinson's patients have been found to suffer from depression related to difficulties in adjusting to the illness or to chemical imbalance caused by the disease, which increases the person's susceptibility to depression (Baldwin and Byrne, 1989), it is possible for the condition to be misinterpreted as dementia.

Parkinsonian symptoms are reduced by treating patients with levodopa (L-dopa), which slows but does not stop the progress of the disease. This medication, taken over a period of time, can cause side-effects which include

Case study 2

Mrs Mercer was a 78-year-old married woman with a three-month history of withdrawal from social activities and a reduction of involvement in shopping and household chores. She reported dizzy spells and had fallen when on a pensioners' club outing.

Mrs Mercer was referred by her GP to the local psycho-geriatrician's out-patient clinic, where she was seen along with her husband and daughter. Mrs Mercer sat motionless throughout the appointment; her movements and response to questions were very slow and her facial expression was mask-like and expressionless. She showed poor concentration and memory for events of the previous few weeks but she did respond clearly and appropriately to questions about her personal and family history. Mrs Mercer's husband and daughter were very concerned and confided that they feared Mrs Mercer was suffering from senile dementia, since a neighbour suffered from this condition and, according to Mr Mercer, 'it started the same way'.

Talking Point: What do you think might be wrong here?

Intervention and outcome

Detailed examination revealed that Mrs Mercer showed cogwheel rigidity (no arm swing on walking), marked tongue tremor, and severe slowness in carrying out motor actions (bradykinesia). These are all signs present in untreated Parkinson's Disease. Mrs Mercer reported that she was sleeping badly, had a poor appetite and was spending a great deal of time worrying about what might be wrong.

It was concluded that she was suffering from idiopathic Parkinson's Disease with depression secondary to this affecting her memory and concentration. Treatment with an anti-Parkinson's drug was prescribed and over the next two months Mrs Mercer became faster at physical tasks, could walk more rapidly and with greater ease, was more cheerful and had started to attend the pensioners' club again. When seen in the out-patients' clinic two months later, Mr and Mrs Mercer reported that she was 'back to her normal self'.

hallucinations and disinhibited behaviour. Careful monitoring of medication is very important, so that any side-effects are identified as early as possible.

Advice on dealing with the worsening of motor symptoms will be helpful to Parkinsonian patients. Occupational, speech and physiotherapists have a role here. Psychological therapy aimed at helping the person to adjust to loss of previous physical fitness and developing appropriate coping strategies can minimise the chance of more severe depression occurring.

Stroke

A cerebrovascular accident (CVA) or 'stroke' as it is more commonly known, occurs as a result of a thrombosis or haemorrhage in the blood vessels leading to the brain or in the vessels of the brain itself. Unlike a transient ischaemic attack (TIA) which can result in a complete recovery at least on the first one or two occasions, a stroke may leave the person with physical problems, the most common of which are changes in muscle tone, leaving paralysis or residual weakness in limbs or on one side of the body; language problems; sight deficits; perceptual problems; personality changes; intellectual and emotional change.

About five in every one thousand people over 65 are affected by stroke. Unlike dementia, recovery of function over time may be possible with stroke patients, particularly if a rehabilitation programme involving early mobilisation of affected limbs is begun early enough. However, as time passes, the restoration of lost functions is increasingly unlikely.

It must be remembered that survivors of stroke will have deficits in some areas but that other areas of functioning and insight into problems will be intact and will remain so. This is often associated with significant motivation and mood disturbances. In addition to physical therapies and appropriate rehabilitation involving the use of other abilities to compensate for deficits, counselling may help with motivation and adjustment problems, as will the support of other survivors (eg. via a Stroke Club). Advice and support for relatives is also needed.

Psychological and Emotional Problems

Depression

Depression is the most common emotional problem affecting older adults. About 30 per cent of people in one survey were found to be moderately or severely depressed (Murphy, 1982). However the condition may be underdiagnosed because symptoms are attributed to other causes. Thus weight loss and fatigue and preoccupation with somatic complaints are put down to physical illness, agitation to anxiety, and problems with thinking and concentration to dementia or sometimes just 'old age'. Table 4.2 lists the symptoms most commonly associated with depression.

Even when the condition has been properly identified, many individuals do not receive treatment with anti-depressants or referral to specialist services (McDonald, 1986). Possible reasons for this include viewing depression in old age as 'normal', believing that psychological problems at this time are inevitable or that older people are rigid in their thinking and will not co-operate with treatment programmes.

Delay in accurate diagnosis and treatment can occur because severe

Table 4.2
Symptoms which
occur in depression

Low mood (sad, irritable, unhappy)	Forgetfulness*
Loss of interest and pleasure	Agitation or retardation of movement*
Sleep disturbance	Loss of energy, tiredness or fatigue*
Weight loss	Feelings of worthlessness and guilt*
Reduction in activity levels	Thinking and concentration disturbances*
Hopelessness	Thoughts of death or suicide*
Helplessness	Preoccupation with somatic complaints*

* Particularly common in the elderly
(table from Hanley and Baikie, 1984).

depression can lead to some of the symptoms found in dementia of the Alzheimer type, such as forgetfulness, poor concentration and slowness in carrying out activities of daily living. The term 'depressive pseudodementia' has been used to describe cases where this has occurred.

Although depression and dementia can be confused, there are certain key differences, outlined in Table 4.3. Of course it is possible for someone to suffer from depression and dementia. Treatment of the depression can lead to considerable improvement in the person's ability to function, even though they are still affected by the problems of the dementing process (*see Chapter 20*).

The person with depression	The person with dementia of the Alzheimer type
Often complains of a poor memory	Is often unaware of memory problems
Will say, "I do not know" in answer to questions which require thought or concentration	Will 'confabulate' or make up answers to questions which require concentration or good memory and appear unaware that the answer is incorrect
Shows fluctuating ability and uneven impairment on cognitive testing	Tends to show consistent, global impairment on cognitive testing
Gives up easily, is poorly motivated and uninterested	Has a go
May be slow but successful in any complex task, aware of errors	Unsuccessful in carrying out tasks which require concentration, appears unaware of errors

Table 4.3
Differences between depression and dementia

Case study 3

Mr Donaldson, aged 71, was a retired car production worker, married, with one daughter and two grandchildren. He had been admitted to hospital because he seemed disorientated, forgetful and was not eating or sleeping properly. His wife reported that he had hardly spoken for a week and had taken to getting up in the night and sitting for hours in the kitchen, staring into space. Staff noticed that Mr Donaldson took a long time to get dressed in the morning and did not wish to join in any group activities, saying he did not know what to do. Mr Donaldson did appear to get a little better as the day progressed and sometimes talked about sports programmes on television with other patients in the evening. The psychologist noticed that, while Mr Donaldson gave up when asked questions which required concentration, he was able to talk more freely when he led the conversation and could provide accurate information on his family, previous work and hobbies when given time. Mr Donaldson complained about having a bad memory, 'being too old to cope', and not being able to support his wife financially.

Talking Point: What do you think might be wrong here?

Intervention and outcome

In discussion with the hospital social worker it emerged that money worries since his retirement six years before had gradually eroded Mr Donaldson's sense of self-esteem, leading him to feel hopeless about remaining independent of state support and gradually giving up all interest in life.

A multidisciplinary approach to treatment, involving financial advice, medication and psychotherapy, enabled Mr Donaldson to regain his self-esteem, his interest in life and his ability to cope with financial problems. Normal eating and sleeping patterns returned and he started to go out on his own to visit old friends and arranged a surprise 'thank-you' party for his wife for supporting him through his difficulties.

Various theories exist to explain the causes of depression, ranging from the view that depression arises as a result of an imbalance in the chemistry of the brain to those which consider that stressful life events like bereavement and loss or the lack of a sense of control over one's environment can bring about depression. In reality it is likely that the cause is multi-factorial. (*See Chapter 20 for more on causes of depression.*)

If the depressed mood remains undetected this may result in severe apathy, withdrawal from life and, in some cases, suicide. Suicides among elderly people are more common than might be supposed, with approximately 25 per cent of all suicides in the United Kingdom being people over 65 years of age (Lindesay, 1986).

While older adults do respond well to anti-depressants, certain side-effects, most notably cardiac arrhythmias and hypertension, have been reported (Baldwin, 1988). In general elderly people have been offered little in the way of counselling or psychotherapy, as the prevailing view has been that they would be unable to look at problems from a psychological point of view and would be resistant to changing the way they think or behave. However, where older adults have been offered psychotherapy and where it has been modified to take physical and psychological issues relevant to the aging process into account, the outcome of treatment is favourable. In some cases elderly patients may improve more than younger people (Knight, 1983).

It is likely that multidisciplinary assessment would be of great benefit and that in many instances a combination of approaches would be most helpful.

Paraphrenia

This condition is often defined as 'schizophrenia of late life'. It occurs in less than 1 per cent of those over the age of 65 and is far less common than schizophrenia among younger people. People with paraphrenia are none the less often known to professionals because the symptoms, which include hallucinations and delusions about being persecuted, can be bizarre and socially disruptive. Calling on neighbours and reporting imagined incidents of theft to the police are not uncommon. The condition tends to occur in deaf, socially isolated people and there may be a sex-linked component, since the majority of sufferers are female.

Carers will notice that the sufferer seems to have confused and disordered thought patterns which tend to focus around ideas of being robbed, spied upon or attacked. The person may imagine voices or misinterpret the function of certain objects. Although in some instances paraphrenic symptoms may be associated with subtle organic changes in the brain and mild impairment of cognitive functioning (Hymas *el al.*, 1989), by and large the condition does improve in response to treatment. Medication tends to be the treatment of choice but some success has been reported with behavioural interventions (Carstensen and Fremouw, 1981).

Family, friends and home care staff have an important role to play in supporting the sufferer. They should be advised on how to deal with the person in a sensitive manner, colluding with rather than confronting their inaccurate statements and suggesting responses which will minimise the chance of the person entering a state of siege (refusing to open the door, throwing away

Case study 4

> Miss Dent, an 80-year-old retired nurse, lived alone in a rented flat. She had little social life apart from fortnightly visits from her niece and weekly trips to a local pensioners' club. She had a home help twice a week because she was partially sighted and needed help around the house. Over a period of eight weeks or so, Miss Dent's home help noticed that she was becoming rather hostile and suspicious. She refused to part with money for groceries which the home help shopped for regularly, saying, "You took all my money yesterday," an accusation which was quite inaccurate. Miss Dent was also quite convinced that people were spying on her through a smoke detector recently installed by the council, and reported this to the police.

Talking Point: What do you think might be helpful to Miss Dent and her carers?

Intervention and outcome

> Miss Dent's home help was concerned and spoke to her home care organiser, who persuaded Miss Dent to allow her doctor to visit. Following assessment by a psychogeriatrician, Miss Dent was treated by means of medication. A community psychiatric nurse (CPN) visited weekly to monitor her mental state and to advise the home help on how to deal with Miss Dent's suspicions without being confrontational. A structure of activities for the week was planned between the CPN and Miss Dent, which meant that she felt active and useful and had less time to focus on her deluded thinking.

meals on wheels) or attacking their supposed aggressor. It is important to be aware that moving house is unlikely to be a solution to the problem of auditory hallucinations, as 'the voice' is likely to move too.

Anxiety

This is sometimes overlooked in older people and symptoms of anxiety, such as palpitations, sweating, butterflies in the stomach, feelings of sickness and diarrhoea, are attributed to physical illness instead of emotional stress. However acute anxiety can lead to panic attacks and hyperventilation (breathing at an abnormally fast rate, which induces dizziness, faintness, tightening in the chest, tingling fingers and toes, head and stomach pains) which can impair concentration and ability to carry out routine tasks just as much as those conditions already mentioned. If left undiagnosed and untreated the sufferer's poor functioning may be put down to declining intellectual abilities.

Attacks of acute anxiety may be associated with particular stressful worries or events which can be clearly identified. In such situations teaching the individual how to use relaxation exercises and anxiety management strategies which involve techniques such as visualising themselves coping with a stressful event can be of great benefit. For those who hyperventilate — Holden (1988) suggests that this is likely to be anyone who breathes at a rate of over 20 breaths per minute when there is no alternative medical reason — strategies should include learning to breathe from the diaphragm rather than the thorax and exercises designed to help slow their breathing down.

Sometimes it is more difficult to find a trigger for anxiety. Thus it may be labelled 'free-floating anxiety'. This tends to be more difficult to treat as the person cannot readily learn strategies to cope with fearful situations. However relaxation may prove fruitful. Tranquillisers may help a great deal in some circumstances, but they are often prescribed as a first treatment rather than a last resort. In most cases it is better to try and help the person to analyse the triggers for their anxiety and explore ways of using relaxation and anxiety management strategies to help them take control of the problem themselves, rather than fostering dependency on potentially addictive benzodiazepines.

Alcohol-related Problems

Other than alcohol-related dementia and Korsakoff's Psychosis, which are mentioned in Chapter 3, intermittent drinking bouts can bring about the confusion and disorientation often associated with dementia. The smell of alcohol in the house of an apparently confused person may require sensitive questioning. Problems associated with drink may arise following a bereavement.

It seems that there is a significant proportion of women who increase their alcohol consumption in their 70s. This may well represent a coping strategy in response to widowhood and loneliness. Even for the man who has drunk two pints a night for years and has been sober afterwards, metabolic changes in later life can mean that alcohol may have a more pronounced effect than it used to.

Sometimes drinking heavily is associated with poor eating habits and, taken together, these can lead to intermittent confusion and, ultimately, physical ill health. If the drinking is a recently adopted coping strategy to handle grief, it may be possible to explore alternatives. Some people may be quite unaware of how little it can take to make them drunk and advice may be helpful. For those unable or unwilling to reduce their consumption it is important that carers are aware that it is drink and not dementia which is causing difficulties and that the person's abilities are likely to fluctuate because of this.

Conclusion

This chapter does not cover all the conditions which may be confused with dementia but attempts to emphasise the importance of excluding other possible conditions rather than jumping to conclusions that dementia is present. Table 4.4 highlights some of the similarities and differences between dementia and the other conditions discussed.

It is important that those involved in providing assessment and support services for dementia sufferers have skills or access to people with skills in differentiating between a dementing process and a condition which may be reversible and require quite a different sort of treatment or intervention.

Problem	Similarities to dementia	Differences from dementia
Acute confusional state	Disorientation, poor concentration, self-neglect	Occurs rapidly, worse at night; disappears after underlying cause treated; clouding of consciousness
Depression	Poor concentration, slowness, non-responsiveness	Answers which are given are usually accurate, but 'do not know' is the frequent response
Anxiety	Inability to carry out day-to-day tasks because of agitation, catastrophic reaction — total failure to cope	No confabulation, insight into impaired functioning; when stressors minimised ability is as normal
Paraphrenia	Misinterpretation of events, actions and statements, self-neglect	Components of behaviour unimpaired, no missing out of steps in a task, even if reasoning seems bizarre; hallucinations
Alcohol problems	Disorientation, 'recent memory' loss, poor co-ordination	Clouded not clear consciousness; problems reduced when sobered up
Parkinson's Disease	Increased dependency, withdrawal from social activity	Abilities and involvement may be improved by medication

Table 4.4 Similarities and differences between dementia and other physical and psychological problems

Problem	Similarities to dementia	Differences from dementia
Stroke	Speech and language problems Motor slowing, poor concentration, withdrawal	Recovery of function possible Deficits not global; insight into loss; can use intact abilities to compensate for deficits

Table 4.4   *(continued)*

REFERENCES

Baldwin R C, 'Late Life Depression: Undertreated?', *British Medical Journal* 296, p 519, 20 Feb. 1988.

Baldwin R C and Byrne E J, 'Psychiatric Aspects of Parkinsons' Disease: Dementia, Depression and Psychosis', *British Medical Journal* 299, pp 3–4, 1 July 1989.

Carstensen L L and Fremouw W J, 'The Demonstration of a Behavioural Intervention for Late Life Paranoia', *Gerontologist* 21, pp 329–33, 1981.

Cummings J L, 'Subcortical Dementia: Neuropsychology, Neuropsychiatry and Pathophysiology, *British Journal of Psychiatry* 149, pp 682–97, 1986.

Hanley I and Baikie E, 'Understanding and Treating Depression in the Elderly', I Hanley and J Hodge (eds), *Psychological Approaches to the Care of the Elderly*, Croom Helm, Beckenham, 1984.

Holden U, *Neuropsychology of Aging*, Croom Helm, Beckenham, 1988.

Hymas N, Naguib M and Levy R, 'Late Paraphrenia; a follow-up study', *International Journal of Geriatric Psychiatry* 4, pp 23–9, 1989.

Knight B G, 'Assessing a mobile outreach team', M A Smyer and M Gatz (eds), *Mental Health and Aging: Programs and Evaluation*, Sage, Beverly Hills, 1983.

Knight R G, Godfrey H P D and Shelton E J, 'The Psychological Deficits Associated with Parkinson's Disease', *Clinical Psychology Review* 8, pp 391–410, 1988.

Lindesay J, 'Suicide and attempted suicide in old age', E Murphy (ed.), *Affective Disorders in the Elderly*, Churchill Livingstone, Edinburgh, 1986.

McDonald A J D, 'Do General Practitioners "miss" Depression in Elderly Patients?', *British Medical Journal* 292, pp 1365–7, 24 May 1986.

Murphy E, 'Social Origins of Depression in Old Age', *British Journal of Psychiatry* 141, pp 135–42, 1982.

PART 2

Discovery

CHAPTER 5   *Fiona Goudie*

Intellectual & Behavioural Assessment

*R*equests for visits by social workers to the homes of elderly individuals, letters from GPs to psychiatrists, community nurses, occupational therapists and other professions are often concluded with statements such as 'Please assess and advise.' Likewise the recommendation following such visits may lead to a further referral to an in-patient unit, occupational or physiotherapy unit or to the staff in a residential home asking for more detailed assessment. But what should we do when we carry out an assessment, and how can it help?

This chapter begins by examining why assessment is important in describing the problems experienced by people with memory, language, concentration and psychomotor problems, who may also have difficulties with activities of daily living, such as cooking, shopping or dressing. It goes on to consider what aspects of an individual's functioning and personal circumstances it might be useful to evaluate and looks at some of the measures which have been developed for professional staff to use. Finally the chapter looks at the issue of dependency and the way direct care staff, including home helps and care assistants, can help to identify needs.

Why Assess?

Increasingly those closely involved in working with older people are aware of the importance of a careful and sensitive assessment. Descriptions of an individual's current ability, as well as an understanding of their previous skills, have an important part to play, for the reasons listed in Table 5.1. Of course

Table 5.1
Reasons for
assessment

- Provides a baseline of functioning against which future improvement or deterioration can be measured
- Contributes to establishing diagnosis
- Makes carers aware of severity of problems
- Provides information on existing level of ability
- Provides families with a comprehensive description of difficulties so they have an awareness of what to expect of their confused relative
- Gives some indication of the level of home support or residential care a person might require in the future

individuals and families sometimes feel concerned about the reason for assessment and may be worried about extensive formal interviews. Sometimes people feel afraid of what may be found out, or feel stupid if they cannot give the day or year or remember their own date of birth. Explaining the function, as outlined in Table 6.1, can often reassure anxious clients or patients and their families.

What to Assess?

The answer to this question often depends on the reason the assessment was sought in the first place. It is important for those seeking assessment to be clear about how they think the information will help them. Possible questions which such a descriptive assessment can help answer include:

- How much is a person able to remember at once?
- How quickly are they able to carry out tasks?
- Can they read and write well enough to be able to cope with bills and pension books?
- What personal details do they remember?
- How well orientated are they?
- How well do they communicate?
- How well can they cook, wash and dress themselves?

Obviously the exact nature of particular questions will depend on the circumstances of the individual. It may be less important to assess someone's cooking skills and ability to cope with bills if they live with a carer than if they live alone and are being considered for a place in a sheltered flat. A home care organiser may be keen to know whether someone is unable to carry out a task or just very slow at it. This may be crucial to understanding the person's dependency level so that appropriate domiciliary support can be arranged. Too much support can de-skill and lead to difficulties just as easily as too little.

It is important that professionals carry out their assessments in a systematic fashion and that the information they collect is meaningful to care-givers. It is impossible to try to examine *why* a problem is occurring unless a clear description of an individual's abilities and experiences is given within an appreciation and evaluation of the wider personal, social and environmental context. Behaviour is shaped by health and handicap, life experiences and living arrangements (the analysis of this is looked at in greater detail in Chapters 7 and 8). Thus a comprehensive assessment should include questions on the areas mentioned in Table 5.2.

Table 5.2
What to assess?

> ■Physical health
> ■Mobility
> ■Mental ability (memory, orientation, language, attention, speed of information processing, ability to carry out voluntary motor actions, such as miming how to clean teeth, drawing and writing)
> ■Daily living skills (for example, shopping, cooking, dressing)
> ■Educational and occupational history
> ■Hobbies and interests
> ■Family composition and social networks
> ■Living situation
> ■Financial situation
> ■Use of services in the statutory, voluntary and private services

How to Assess?

Although informal assessment of a person's abilities is important and much can be learned from talking to clients and their carers in an unstructured way, sometimes crucial items are missed out and the discussion focusses on problems at the expense of strengths.

Professionals working in assessment teams, whether these are based in community, day, residential or hospital settings, should adopt a brief, semi-structured interview style which will help identify the need for more detailed assessment in certain areas. Various assessment schedules exist to provide a preliminary descriptive profile of the individual's functioning and the nature of their surroundings which can help establish whether a more detailed investigation is necessary or not. Table 5.3 lists some of these measures.

Descriptions of accommodation may highlight an inaccessible toilet and lead to a detailed occupational therapy (OT) assessment, while early morning waking, poor appetite and tearfulness may suggest that further examination of mood would be valuable. Additionally, this structured description may prevent professionals jumping to conclusions about causes when they have insufficient information. An assessment of orientation, memory, language ability, concentration and motor functions may suggest the presence of a dementing process. However, if the person's educational and occupational history revealed that they

Table 5.3
Assessment

Assessment measure	Type of information obtained
Clifton Assessment Procedures for the Elderly (CAPE)	Cognitive functioning and behaviour
Geriatric Depression Scale (GDS) Beck Depression Inventory (BDI)	Depressed mood Depressed mood
Crichton Geriatric Rating Scale	Behaviour
Lawton and Brody's Instrumental Activities of Daily Living (IADL)	Food preparation, laundry, financial responsibility
Holden's Orientation Facilities Checklist (ORIF)	Architecture and sensory stimulation

were always bottom of the class and could never read properly, then it may be that the 'deterioration' is not recent but an indication of low educational attainment or intellectual ability. Clinical psychologists can carry out specialised assessments which estimate a person's pre-morbid level of intellectual functioning.

Dependency Levels

Much attention has been paid recently to the importance of establishing levels of dependency among dementia sufferers. This is helpful in determining the kinds of support and treatment a person may require in their own home as well as planning the service needs for a group of people in a particular setting (eg. a hospital ward or residential home). However it must be borne in mind that dependency ratings are an aggregate score of behavioural excesses (eg. aggression, repetition) and deficits (eg. an unwillingness to dress or bathe). They do not in themselves identify individual need.

Much of the work on establishing levels of dependency is in the early stages of development. The Clifton Assessment Procedures for the Elderly (CAPE) is one measure which has been researched extensively and for which dependency ratings have been derived from scores on cognitive and behavioural tests. It has been tested out in many settings, and has been shown to help reliably with diagnosis, estimating deterioration and establishing dependency levels of individuals.

Of course it is important to treat the use of dependency ratings with caution because the factors contributing to them vary widely and may indicate the need for different management strategies. A person may have a 'high dependency' rating as a result of depression or mobility problems. If these are treated the person's rating may fall into the 'low dependency' category. On the other hand, a person with dementia may have a moderate dependency score at present, but this score may reflect difficulties which are unlikely to be remediable in the long term. Ultimately the person may have 'high dependency' needs. A comprehensive, descriptive assessment can help to indicate exactly those areas which contribute to a person's need for help or treatment. It is equally important to take strengths and abilities into account. These can be used to enable the person to cope with their difficulties. Chapter 10, on goal planning, expands on the way this can be achieved.

Conclusion

The assessment measures outlined in this chapter are the starting-point in the identification of a possible dementing process. They describe the person's abilities and life circumstances but do not explain why a particular ability is affected or why a particular problem is occurring.

The next four chapters in this part of the book move on from a description of *what* is happening to develop an analysis of *why* problems may occur and *how* organic change and other factors can influence behaviour.

FURTHER READING

Beck A T, Ward C, Mendelson M, Mock J E and Erbaugh J, 'An inventory for measuring depression', *Archives of General Psychiatry* 42, pp 142–8, 1961.

Gallagher D, Nies G and Thompson L, 'Reliability of the Beck Depression Inventory with older adults', *Journal of Consulting and Clinical Psychology* 50, pp 152–3, 1982.

Holden U, *Thinking it Through*, Winslow Press, Bicester, 1984.

Lawton M P and Brody E M, 'Assessment of older people: self-maintaining and instrumental activities of daily living', *Gerontologist* 9, pp 179–86, 1969.

Pattie A H and Gilleard C J, *Manual of the Clifton Assessment Procedures for the Elderly (CAPE)*, Hodder & Stoughton, Sevenoaks, 1979.

Robinson R A, 'Differential Diagnosis and Assessment in Brain Failure', *Age and Aging* 6, pp 42–9 (Supplement on Crichton Geriatric Rating Scale), 1977.

Yesavage J and Brink T L, 'Development and Validation of a Geriatric Depression Screening Scale: A preliminary report', *Journal of Psychiatric Research* 17, pp 37–49, 1983.

Dementia: Some Common Misunderstandings

We can all misunderstand others, jump to conclusions and make false assumptions. When working with patients, particularly those who are confused, it is wise to tread carefully.

Neuropsychology is the study of the relationship between the brain and behaviour. Unfortunately it is omitted from most training programmes for professionals. The term is off-putting, but some familiarity with the subject is vital to all working with confused elderly people, as it can supply relevant information as to the origin and nature of certain behaviours. Moreover the formulation of a relevant plan of therapeutic management and rehabilitation and its skilful implementation can be facilitated by the knowledge that particular behavioural difficulties implicate specific areas of brain damage.

Misinterpretation of Behaviour

As with the jargon used by engineers, musicians, gardeners and most other special interest groups, the language of neuropsychology is strange until it is explained. When you come across the prefixes 'a' or 'dys', they simply mean 'disorder of . . .'

Aphasia is an impairment of language, often simply implying speech (ie expressive aphasia) though really including reading, writing and number, as well as comprehension (ie receptive aphasia). Word-finding difficulty is known as *anomia. Agraphia* specifically refers to writing disorders, *alexia* to reading and *acalculia* to number problems.

Apraxia concerns movement disorders which are not due to physical deficits. The person is capable of making the movement, can perform the actions without thinking, but runs into trouble when trying consciously to perform the action or task. Dressing apraxia means that the almost automatic system for dressing oneself has been lost. Brain damage in the non-dominant parietal and occipital lobes (*see Figure 6.1*) results in the person being unable to relate

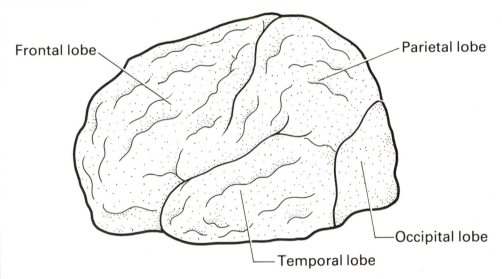

Figure 6.1
Major divisions of
the human cerebral
cortex as viewed
from the side

Hemisphere: the human cerebral cortex is divided into right and left hemispheres.

Dominant Hemisphere: the hemisphere that is more important in the comprehension and production of speech is referred to as the 'dominant' hemisphere; it is usually the left hemisphere, especially in right-handed people.

Lobe: each hemisphere is divided into four areas, each known as a lobe: frontal, temporal, parietal and occipital. The division of the lobes is based partly on anatomical factors and partly on functional aspects.

themselves to their clothing, so clothes are put on in the wrong order, upside down, back-to-front, etc.

Agnosias are related to disorders of recognition. They result in an inability to identify an object by sight alone, speech or sound by hearing alone, and so on. Visual agnosia is not only an inability to name or demonstrate the use of an object without touching it, but also a lack of recognition of the object's meaning or character. The person does not even remember seeing anything like it before. Interesting variations of visual agnosia:

Spatial agnosia, an inability to find the way around even familiar places, is a disorientation in space not produced by memory impairment.

Prosopagnosia is an inability to recognise familiar faces. A familiar voice often resolves the difficulty.

Simultanagnosia is an inability to recognise writing or pictorial material as a whole; only parts can be recognised.

Anosognosia, or one-side neglect (usually the left side), is a fairly common dysfunction which is sometimes the result of a stroke. The person may not 'see' their own body as a whole and may deny that their left hand belongs to them.

All parts of the brain have roles to play in conjunction with other parts in the

Table 6.1
Frontal signs

- ■Perseveration (ie repetition) of words, phrases or actions
- ■Perseveration of thought could be called the 'stuck needle syndrome', as the person gets stuck with a subject, and is unable to move from it
- ■Inability to deal with abstract thought: for example, a person will find it hard to grasp the meaning of sayings such as 'A rolling stone gathers no moss', their explanation being quite literal
- ■Difficulty in understanding others' viewpoints
- ■Inability to put events or actions into a logical order
- ■Impulsivity, poor judgement, mood swings
- ■Inability to learn from experience
- ■Difficulty in monitoring own behaviour

production of behaviour, although there appear to be areas of specific localised function. Speech is usually centred in the left hemisphere. Appreciation of space is associated with the parietal lobes. However it is the frontal region that is of special interest to those working with confused elderly people, as damage here can result in troublesome behaviour. Table 6.1 lists the signs of frontal lobe damage. Not all of these problems will be present in each patient; the degree of deficit and the extent of behavioural problems will vary from person to person.

Understanding

Before jumping to conclusions, careful observations should be recorded and simple tasks given to see how the person responds:

- Can the person read a magazine or newspaper?
- Is comprehension good?
- Are famous faces recognised?
- Are colours identified?
- Can the person read from left to right, or only one side of the page?
- Can the person count?
- Can the person write?
- Can tasks be performed on request?
- Are relatives recognised by face, or only when they speak?
- Are staff similarly recognised?
- Is the mirror image of self recognised?
- What is the person's speech like?
- Can the person find their way around?
- Is an established interest or hobby now poorly practised?

This is only a simple screening method. It cannot provide a clear-cut picture, but it can help to avoid misinterpretations such as are shown in Table 6.2.

Behaviour	Frequent Explanations	Neuropsychological Possibility
Dropping things	Clumsy	Apraxia, possibly due to stroke
Getting into someone else's bed	Over-sexed, lonely, disorientated	Spatial agnosia, or anosognosia
Able to sing, but will not talk	Unco-operative, attention-seeking	Aphasic; rhythm, melody etc preserved
Not always recognising speech or perhaps sounds	Going deaf, being difficult	Possible auditory agnosia
Unable to recognise objects	Going blind	Visual agnosia
Unable to dress self	Lazy, attention-seeking, senile	Dressing apraxia
Repetition of words, phrases or actions	Senile	Frontal damage: perseveration
Walks into things	Forgetful, blind	Anosognosia
Claims to have been assaulted	Troublemaker	Anosognosia
Does not recognise faces	Apathetic, blind	Prosopagnosia: inability to recognise faces

These are just a few examples of behaviours that can be misunderstood.

Table 6.2 Possible misinterpretations and alternative explanations

Case Examples of Neuropsychological Problems

Mr Peter Frame is the centre of controversy. His relatives have taken out an action against the staff, as he claims that one of them punched him in the stomach during the night. Other patients resent him as he gets into their beds and sits on top of them at mealtimes.

Miss Ellie Waters seems to be 'acting up'. Her constant repetitions irritate everyone, then she suddenly responds as if to a question when she is told to be quiet. Eventually someone notices that the question had been asked about 15 minutes previously.

Mrs Mary Peach was once sociable, intelligent and active, but after her husband's death she became uninterested and very dependent on her daughter. A small stroke was suspected, but there was no clear evidence, so she was admitted to hospital for investigations. Her condition apparently deteriorated; the staff washed, dressed and fed her, only to notice, one day, that, while she sat on her own watching television, she was brushing her hair and drinking a cup of tea.

Think about possible neuropsychological explanations before reading further.

Interpretation

Mr Frame's anosognosia causes him to be unaware of people, things or events to one side of him. As a result he gets into the bed he sees, mistakes his own hand touching his body for that of another and fails to see someone sitting on chairs to the neglected side.

Miss Waters, on the other hand, has frontal lobe damage. Her mind is stuck on a line of thought preventing messages getting through. Eventually someone 'lifts the needle' when she is interrupted, and she gives an appropriate answer, even if the response is much delayed. Apart from perseveration she may also have a degree of aphasia, which adds to her difficulties.

Mrs Peach has an apraxia which means that she experiences difficulties when she attempts to perform self-care activities when these efforts are under conscious control following instructions. Telling her what to do adds to her confusion. To tell her to 'pick up your knife and fork' will always prove unhelpful.

Conclusion

The aim of this chapter is to provoke thought as to the nature of brain–behaviour relationships in dementia. When setting treatment or management goals it is important to realise that many behaviours could be the result of specific impairments of brain function. By working together staff may well find answers to puzzling difficulties and discover good practical ways to solve the challenging behaviour.

FURTHER READING

Holden U P, *Looking at Confusion*, Winslow Press, Bicester, 1987.
Holden U P (ed.), *Neuropsychology and Aging*, Croom Helm, London, 1988.
Holden U P and Woods R T, *Reality Orientation: Psychological Approaches to the 'Confused' Elderly*, Churchill Livingstone, Edinburgh, 1988.
Jorm A F, *Understanding Senile Dementia*, Croom Helm, London, 1987.

Seeking an Explanation

What is Happening?

Chapter 5 described some 'user-friendly' assessment measures which provide an accurate descriptive 'snapshot' of an aged person's behaviour and life circumstances. Chapter 6 outlined the behavioural consequences of certain types of neurological damage. Both focus on clarifying *what* may be happening and may be used to develop effective intervention to resolve difficulties and develop remaining strengths.

However it is all too common for a single assessment instrument or examination to be used in isolation to identify *why* a person is dependent, disruptive or unable to function within their surroundings. The identification during assessment of, for example, a behavioural deficit or excess does not enable the observer to discriminate between presumed underlying causes. A single test cannot provide information as to *why* behaviour is occurring. It tells us *what* is happening in a specific area of function and ability.

As Chapter 5 outlined, the influences on behaviour are varied. Many factors have to be taken into account when establishing why something is happening. The process of diagnosis is the pulling together of information from a range of assessment measures and investigations in order to establish probable cause. The objective is to achieve a dynamic picture of the whole person and their fit within the environment which explains why deterioration is a feature of late life.

Even when an overall assessment of the person yields a diagnosis of dementia it is wrong to assume that any behavioural change, intellectual deficit or disturbance of mood observed in a dementing person must inevitably be the result of the cerebral disease. Such an attitude generates hopelessness and pessimism amongst carers: nothing can be done, their condition is destined to deteriorate, so what is the point in bothering with ideas of 'treatment' and rehabilitation.

Fortunately, in dementia the origins of behaviour remain complex. So much more still needs to be considered when developing an understanding of behaviour than simply that this person is dementing. A model of the multiple pathway to behaviour clearly illustrates this.

The Multiple Pathway to Behaviour

Behaviour (this term covers thought, mood, speech and action, and is not being used to refer solely to observable movement as in everyday parlance), is influenced by biogenic (ie physical health and handicap), psychogenic (ie personality and personal history) and environmental factors. Figure 7.1 shows how each of these pathways needs to be considered when an explanation is sought as to why a dementing elderly person is displaying a particular behaviour or loss of ability.

The biogenic pathway

Examination and investigation of a person's physical status must involve an accurate diagnosis of the presence, extent and severity of dementia. Too often the label of dementia enters a case history on the basis of imprecise personal opinions based solely on an interview with the 'sufferer'. Recently one of the authors came across a case of an able Polish gentleman in his late 80s who had been diagnosed as suffering from dementia in 1953, following an interview on admission to the local psychiatric hospital!

Table 7.1 illustrates a model of good diagnostic practice. If such procedures have not been implemented, then the reliability of the diagnosis may legitimately be questioned.

In addition, the way we act is influenced by how healthy we feel. It is difficult to perform well when suffering from a cold or distracted by a raging toothache. Similarly, our ability to function is affected by the quality of our senses, physical strength and ability to perform and co-ordinate movement. There is need to examine the aged person so that illness and pain, physical and sensory handicaps and medication side-effects can be excluded as reasons for impaired performance (*see Case Study page 63*). It must always be borne in mind that the confused, intellectually damaged, speech impaired dementia

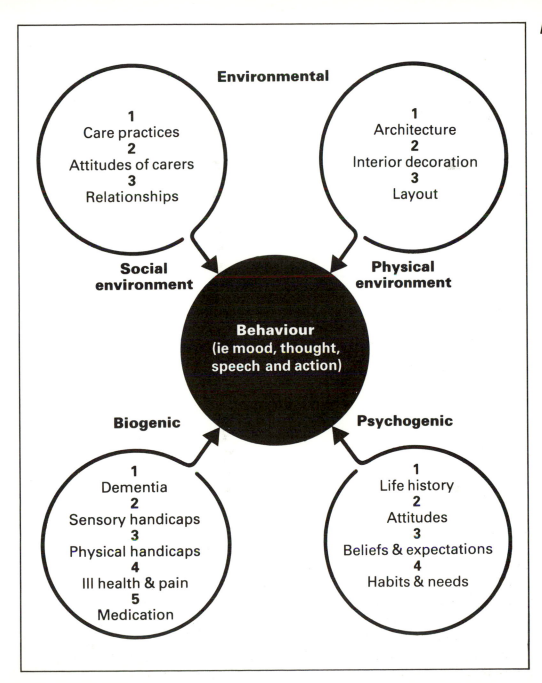

Figure 7.1 The holistic model of behavioural determination

Table 7.1
Establishing a
diagnosis of
dementia

1. Systematic assessment of intellectual and behavioural performance over time.

2. A neuropsychological examination of cognitive functions, eg. memory, language, praxis, perception, reasoning.

3. Observation of mental state to include demeanour, mood, speech, thought content and perceptual disturbance.

4. A physical examination to include blood pressure, Central Nervous System (CNS) examination, examination of sight and hearing, and assessment of gait.

5. Laboratory investigations, eg. a full blood count, urea and electrolyte profile, tests of thyroid and liver function, vitamin B12 and folate levels, VDRL (Venereal Disease Reference Laboratory Slide Test — in order to exclude a diagnosis of tertiary syphilis) and blood sugar levels.

6. Radiological investigation, eg. computerised tomography (CT) scans.

7. A history which is as full as possible needs to be obtained from the patient. In addition, an informant should give an account of the patient's pre-morbid intellectual attainments, personality and social functioning, as well as current behaviour patterns and competence. The collection of both historical data and the testimony of independent observers is essential in the discrimination of dementia from other disorders. For example, particular note would be taken of a history of head injury or drug use.

sufferer is unlikely to be able to give articulate expression as to the effect of ill health, handicap and medication. All that will be observed will be a change in behaviour. For example, is the irritable, sullen gentleman who is uncharacteristically tormenting the person next to him suffering from a toothache or indigestion?

The psychogenic pathway

All practitioners regard themselves as individuals with a history, life-style and characteristics unique to them. So why is it so often the case that a dementing

Mrs Ivy Williams is a 74-year-old woman who was referred by her GP for day-hospital assessment. She presented as extremely confused. This was complicated by apparent visual hallucinations.

Medical assessment showed that Mrs Williams was taking a great number of different medications for a variety of comparatively minor ailments. Physical examination identified a history of transient ischaemic attacks (TIAs), suggesting a multi-infarct dementia (MID). Neuropsychological examination revealed a cognitive profile supportive of such a diagnosis.

However, when medication was reduced to a minimum (*see Chapter 22*), the hallucinations disappeared and confusion lessened. A reassessment of behaviour resulted in Mrs Williams remaining at home with her husband, with the support of a home help and regular day care.

person is regarded by professional carers as having homogenous needs and preferences common to 'the confused elderly', to which can be applied uniform measures of care and occupation? It is not the case that, on receipt of a diagnosis of dementia, one acquires a label and discards one's individuality. Whilst personality will be eroded as this devastating disease follows its remorseless path of destruction, it is a gradual, uneven process destined to take a period of years. Therefore, when establishing why particular behaviours are occurring, it is imperative that account is taken not only of the dementing person's world of attitudes, desires and preferences, but also of a life history which has shaped actions and needs observed in late life. Consideration should also be given to the way a person has adjusted to, and coped with, life change and stress.

To neglect this pathway can mean that behaviour is influenced by psychological factors of which staff are unaware. For example, is aggression being triggered by a denial of long-established rituals and habits? Was the resistant patient once a proud and independent person who held a position of authority, and who now resents being told what to do? The message must inevitably be 'know the person', otherwise the provision of care is unlikely to meet individual need.

The environmental pathway

We all act differently in differing settings. We are not expected, nor would it be well received, to act at work as we do at home. Similarly, our behaviour is different when talking to a senior work colleague than it would be when holding a conversation with a close friend. Most of us have experienced the unpleasant feelings of being lost in an unfamiliar and possibly strange environment. Determined efforts are made to make sense of the surroundings by acquiring information. Only when the unfamiliar ceases to be so do feelings of anxiety and concern disappear, and our behaviour appears calm and settled. Those of us who have had the misfortune to require in-patient medical treatment will appreciate how easy it is to be seduced by the routines and dependency relationships characteristic of hospital wards, and then to feel ill at ease when returning home to a life of responsibility and independence. Thus environment and environmental experiences shape behaviour and are a significant dimension of the multiple pathway to behaviour.

When seeking a complete explanation of dementing behaviour, environmental influences cannot be dismissed as irrelevant. It is not the case that dementing people are unaware of their surroundings and thus immune to environmental effects. Issues of environmental design and quality are important considerations for those working with dementia. Serious behavioural deterioration can occur if a dementing person lives in unsupportive surroundings. Inadequate living arrangements and unwise management procedures can bring about unnecessary dependency and the onset of disruptive behaviours. A picture of accelerating decline may give rise to an impression of a rapidly progressing dementia, when it is environmental issues which need to be the focus of attention.

The environment possesses two dimensions, the physical and the social. The physical environment refers to architecture, building design, furnishings and the layout of the interior. Some of the environmental features which do not help the dementing person in their struggle to survive in the face of declining skills and advancing intellectual devastation are discussed in Chapter 9.

The social environment refers to the human world: the people who support and live with the confused person. Thus we are now talking about relationships, the attitudes of carers, care practices and the timetabling of these practices. A poor relationship between a carer and a dementing relative may generate a spiral of behavioural decline. As the former becomes increasingly intolerant and rejecting, so the latter attempts to manipulate and gain attention through becoming increasingly dependent. Conversely, a desire on the part of an involved and loving companion to maintain standards of appearance and cleanliness may not only de-skill the dementing person but also lead to 'difficult' behaviour as attempts are made to assert independence.

An impoverished environment which provides minimal personal contact and little stimulation will lead to withdrawn, listless behaviour. As involvement with social reality diminishes, confusion increases and behaviour rapidly deteriorates.

Conclusion

This chapter has shown that the origins of behaviour are complex and thus cannot be readily identified. It is also likely that a dynamic interplay of underlying forces will exist. For example, the design of a building may have an effect on care practices, while the attitude of carers may be reflected in their use of medication.

In addition, it is probable that confused elderly people will suffer from several difficulties at the same time. Thus, in the pursuit of understanding, there may be a need to disentangle the multiple pathway. Furthermore any interaction between behaviours will also need to be established. For example, the withdrawn and subdued person may be suffering from depression, and it is such an emotion as this which is responsible for an increase in dependent behaviour and passive responses. Over time, dependency may not only become the focus of concern for care-givers, with a corresponding neglect of emotions, but exaggerated incompetence may serve to further darken the dementing person's mood. Apart from interaction effects, certain behaviours may be mediated by others, as when the non-recognition of a partner leads to aggression following intimate contact, or when agitation following separation results in 'wandering' as searching for the loved one takes place.

While the initial response may be to feel overwhelmed by the task of unravelling underlying causes, successful identification of the factors involved can lead to behavioural improvement which is of benefit both to sufferers and carers. Where there was once only pessimism and helplessness there now can be found hope and positive expectations.

CHAPTER 8 — *Graham Stokes*

Behavioural Analysis

*H*aving established the complexity of behaviour, a technology is required which brings order to the information obtained and structures it in such a way that appropriate intervention is indicated. These objectives can be achieved through use of behavioural analysis, often referred to as an **ABC** analysis of behaviour.

Behaviour

All behaviour is unique to the individual, and so it is not possible to think in terms of *group* behaviours (eg. confused elderly, attention-seekers, wanderers) as the basis for responding to *personal* need. A person can also produce the same behaviour at different times for different reasons. So, to gain a genuine understanding of an elderly person's behaviour, it needs to be appreciated as it is occurring *now*. The reasons for a previous episode of toileting difficulty may differ from those which are relevant now, so it is rarely wise to base an opinion solely on a client's previous history.

'Target' Behaviour

The first objective is to determine which of the assessed behaviours is going to be the focus of a behavioural analysis. While it may be tempting to conduct an assault on all problem behaviours this is not a wise strategy. The probable outcome will be chaotic and inconsistent care practice, overwhelmed and disillusioned staff who see themselves as failing to achieve positive change, and an increasingly distressed and confused elderly person who is subject to a variety of imposed demands and limitations. It is advisable to choose a single behaviour in order that a thorough understanding of this 'target' behaviour is achieved. The trap to avoid is being unable to 'see the wood for the trees'.

Another reason for selecting a single client difficulty is that the successful resolution of a problem behaviour can have favourable knock-on effects in so much as other behaviours may also benefit. For example, the positive reaction of others when a self-care goal is achieved may encourage other dormant skills to be resurrected. There may also be a general improvement in social responsiveness. Thus it is not necessary to view every excess or deficit as inevitably requiring independent attention.

Finally, consideration should also be given to whether the most troublesome behaviour should be the initial target for analysis and possible intervention. To show staff and client that change can occur, it can be wise to choose a relatively 'soft' target. It is more than likely that some carers will need to be convinced that 'dementing' behaviour can change as a consequence of their own actions. A minor success can motivate staff and wherever possible clients, to establish additional re-learning goals (*see Chapter 10*), thereby fostering a climate of positive expectation.

Behavioural Analysis

To understand why an elderly person is either expressing an excessive dependency need or displaying an undesirable disruptive behaviour you need to look at the times and situations in which it occurs; who was with or near the confused person at the time; what the person was doing immediately before the target behaviour was observed; and to identify the response of carers (and, if appropriate, other residents or patients) to the incident. These tasks can easily be carried out by following the *ABC analysis of behaviour*:

A = Activating event or situation

B = Behaviour

C = Consequences

If we take aggression as an example, questions which need to be answered under these headings are:

A At what time did the aggression occur?
  When and where did the outburst occur?

What was the person doing immediately before the aggressive outburst?
What was the victim doing prior to the incident?
What was happening around the aggressor at the time?

B   It is important to provide a precise definition of the target behaviour. There is a need to avoid 'fuzzy', imprecise statements. For example, to say to a staff group that we are going to record Mr Lukic's difficult behaviour or that we are going to monitor Mrs Dixon's untidy appearance is a pointless declaration. The descriptions are too vague and subject to individual interpretation. For example, what is difficult to one person may not be to another. What is required is an *operational definition* which precisely details the behaviour to be observed and recorded. The procedure is to get the staff group to 'brainstorm' what is meant by the terms 'aggressive', 'untidy', 'lazy' etc, and then to draw up an operational definition based on the agreed description of the behaviour. For example:

i)   *Physical aggression*   If Mr Lukic should attempt to or actually strike, hit, slap, kick, punch or use (or throw) an object to hit another person this is to be recorded.

ii)   *Verbal abuse*   If Mr Lukic is abusive towards, or shouts at, another person in a threatening manner this is to be recorded.

As can be seen, an operational definition keeps personal opinion and interpretation to a minimum.

When providing information on Behaviour (B) you take advantage of the operational definition and use precise descriptions. For example:
Was the aggressor hitting, kicking, slapping or punching another person?
Who was the victim?
Was an object thrown at the victim?
Was the aggressor causing malicious damage to an object?
Was the aggressor making threatening gestures?
Was the confused aggressor verbally abusive or making threats?
Was the aggressive outburst a temper tantrum?
Was the person agitated or distressed while acting out their aggression?
Were they saying anything during the aggressive incident?

C   What was the response of carers to the aggression?

Was the aggressor comforted, told off, confronted, ignored, sedated or restrained?

What was the aggressor's response to the approach of carers to the violent situation?

What was the reaction of the victim to the attack?

What was the reaction of other residents?

The ABCs are recorded each time an incident is observed. All staff should be aware that the behaviour is being monitored. It is important that the information is recorded as near to the time of the incident as possible, as it is easy to forget the exact circumstances if recording is left until later. Vital information may be omitted if there is a delay.

The collection of all this information on possible contributory factors can be displayed on a record chart similar to that below.

Date & Time	A	B	C	Background

The *Background* column covers information which enables you to place the ABCs in a situational context. For example, has anything happened during the day (or night) which may have caused upset, annoyance or excitement? Has there been a recent change in routine? Has the elderly person recently moved to new surroundings? Is the person on any medication? Has there been a change in medication? Does the resident appear in pain?

If this type of information is not collected then essential reasons for why **B** may be occurring, as well as why the person was in situation **A**, and why they reacted at **C** in the manner they did, will be missed. For example, Mrs Adams may have assaulted the driver of the bus on the way to her first attendance at day care, not primarily because of anything that happened on the vehicle, but because of poor preparation prior to her departure.

A behavioural analysis provides an accurate and detailed description of actual behaviour in terms of how often it occurred, the circumstances in which it arose, the consequences for the elderly confused person, as well as any relevant background occurrences. The information obtained should be shared with all carers, mentioned at 'handover' reports, and discussed during staff meetings.

The Procedure

The observation and recording of the target behaviour should take place over a period of one to two weeks in order to avoid making decisions on the basis of short-term fluctuations in responses. In other words, monitoring for just a few days may result in staff having unwittingly chosen a couple of good days or a particularly bad patch, thereby giving rise to misleading conclusions.

This stage of the behavioural analysis is known as the *baseline* period. It helps not only to identify whether a consistent pattern exists, but also the *frequency* of the target behaviour: that is, how many times target behaviour occurred during the baseline period. Sometimes it is the case that, if the challenging behaviour is observed to have a low frequency, this provides evidence that carers have *lost perspective*. Being confronted by a tiresome difficulty can sap energy, erode tolerance and, as a result, appear unremitting. However, when the low frequency is discussed by staff, they may conclude that the behaviour is not a significant difficulty warranting special attention.

If a genuine problem exists, the frequency recorded forms the baseline against which future changes are measured. Following intervention the frequency of the target behaviour continues to be recorded so that success can be confirmed or denied. Success is a meaningful reduction in frequency, not the ideal of zero frequency.

If there are no positive developments, the management approach requires re-examination. Thus the continued use of frequency recording does away with subjective impressions of whether improvement has occurred or not.

The Person

While the collection of ABCs provides us with a detailed description of the way the environment impacts upon an individual (in a way that a general environmental assessment instrument such as the Orientation Facilities Checklist (Holden, 1984), could never do), it does not give us information on the biogenic and psychogenic pathways. These pathways may be exerting a powerful control over behaviour and may contain the foundations upon which future management and rehabilitation can be established. For example, is there a requirement to compensate for physical handicap and infirmity? Are care plans corresponding to individual need? These questions can only be answered with reference to the biogenic and psychogenic pathways. Therefore, in addition to the **ABC** record charts, a cover sheet providing information on (a) physical health and handicap, and (b) life history and personality, is also needed.

Under *physical health and handicap*, information on the following is covered: the extent and severity of dementia; mobility and dexterity; ill health and chronic pain; medication. In order to obtain a comprehensive *personal history* and description of *personality*, not only care staff and community workers need to be involved in the information-gathering process, but so do the family of the confused person. Questions which may be pertinent when considering the problem of aggression include:

- Are long-established personal routines and habits being denied?
- Would you expect the elderly person to find living with others in a confined space annoying?
- Did the aged person always resent being told what to do?
- Did they have a reputation for being surly, abusive or having a fiery temper?

As a general 'rule' an appreciation of the person should also include information on remaining strengths, as these may be the critical foundations for future change.

When all the areas of information have been collected and the observations have yielded a wealth of situational data, it is the role of the staff group to discuss the findings and identify the critical determinants. Only then can care staff move to the next stage, which is to respond to client need through the introduction of appropriate goal-setting (*see Chapter 10*).

Conclusion

While seeking an explanation can be a lengthy process, taking the trouble to understand a person's behaviour can save valuable time later. If we intervene too quickly with inadequate information about the person and their problem, this may not only be unhelpful, but is likely to result in the situation assuming crisis proportions.

Even when time is not on our side, and staffing levels do not allow for a rigorous period of monitoring, the ABC approach to behavioural difficulties can impose a structure on our thinking which enables us to understand what may be triggering and maintaining the behaviour and guide us towards appropriate intervention.

This approach to understanding problem behaviour can be taught to families of dementia sufferers. While community professionals need to be realistic in what supporters can achieve, given that many will be elderly and frail themselves, talking about and looking at problems within the ABC framework can help relatives to appreciate why difficulties are arising at home. This in itself may be seen as a positive step of significance, even though the problem behaviour may ultimately remain unresolved.

REFERENCE

Holden U, *Thinking it Through*, Winslow Press, Bicester, 1984.

The Environmental Context

*O*ne of the most disappointing and frustrating consequences of conducting a behavioural analysis is to identify the reasons for a client's difficulty, only to find the solution is out of reach. While it may be possible to reveal the situational factors involved in triggering and maintaining behavioural deficits and excesses, wider *contextual* issues may be of greater significance. Features of the home or institutional environment may create the circumstances responsible for the situational causes and in turn may obstruct desired remedial intervention.

Looking beyond the 'limited' view of the environment identified in a behavioural analysis so as to take into account contextual influences is known as 'behavioural ecology'. To change behaviour a fundamental restructuring of the overall environmental setting may be required.

Institutional Care

Social environment

Features of the care system which merit consideration when investigating the reason why difficult and dependent behaviours arise are:

1   Staffing levels. It may not be possible to meet the many needs of residents or patients with existing numbers of staff. Elderly confused people do not have solely physical requirements: they have emotional and social needs which, if neglected, may result in disruptive and dependent behaviour. Some may have activity needs which can only be met by the provision of occupation

(*see Chapter 16*). Without such opportunity to be active the person may despair as they endure an idle and pointless existence.

2   Staff quality. As described in Chapter 1, staff must want to work with dementia sufferers and be knowledgeable about the nature and meaning of dementia. Lack of interest is not an attitude compatible with the delivery of sensitive care. It is often the case that quality care is found, not in establishments rich in material resources, but in those where staff are enthusiastic, committed and informed.

3   Staff rotation. When staff are rotated out of units or wards in either an unpredictable or ever-changing manner, care practices are inconsistent, programmes of rehabilitation are unlikely to be followed and meaningful relationships with clients are not established. However it is just as important to avoid *staff stagnation*, a situation where staff have difficulty in evaluating their practice and accepting change because of an unquestioning and complacent attitude towards established custom and routine born out of years of working in the same setting.

4   Staff morale. Disillusioned, dissatisfied staff are unable to respond sensitively to client need and to create environmental quality. Poor staffing levels, limited career prospects and inadequate training opportunities make staff feel undervalued and generate negative work attitudes. Indices of low staff morale are high levels of sickness, absenteeism and turnover.

5   Task-orientated care. Such an approach creates a belief that staff have 'done a good job' and are valued when they have performed specified tasks, many of which are to do with the smooth running and presentation of the service. Examples of task-orientated care would be allocating priority to such activity as making beds or tidying away after mealtimes. Preoccupation with these activities detracts from building relationships with clients. When activities are person-related, they tend to be conducted on a basis of 'doing something for someone' (for example, toileting, dressing).

6   Rules and regulations. If an establishment is dominated by rules governing everyday activity, not only is the outcome to treat elderly people as a homogeneous group, but the regulations are likely to have been adopted to ensure the 'efficient' running of the organisation, not in order to meet the needs of a disparate group of people. It is as if the needs of the institution predominate over those of the patients or residents they are meant to serve.

In many cases it is not a case of rules but entrenched custom and practice. The following case example illustrates how a regulated system of care can result in an unnecessary increase in dependent behaviour.

Setting	Part III elderly persons' home.
Presenting problem	High dependency needs.
Presumed cause	Dementia sufferers inappropriately placed in a residential setting.

Intervention

Assessment	Observation confirmed impoverished self-care skills.
Analysis	The regulations dictated that residents needed to be washed and dressed by breakfast at 8.00 am. To ensure this goal was achieved staff behaved with minimal regard for individual need, dressing people who actually only required time and assistance.
Conclusion	A de-skilled population of aging residents suffering from a degree of physical frailty and mental infirmity, but, more significantly, living in a regimented, unsupportive environment.

7   Night-time environment. At night inadequate staffing levels, the recruitment of poor-quality, inexperienced night-shift workers and the presence of ill-informed staff who are unaware of daytime care plans exercise an adverse effect on the well-being of residents and patients. The neglect of staff needs in terms of inadequate rest facilities, unpleasant working conditions and low professional status further undermines the provision of quality care.

Table 9.1 illustrates common features of life within an institutional setting which result from a deficient social environment.

Table 9.1
Quality of life in
institutional care

> ■**Loss of occupation and activity**
> 'Doing nothing' appears to be the norm. However, group living units have the lowest levels of inactivity.
>
> ---
>
> ■**An erosion of independent thought and action**
> Independence is often discouraged in the pursuit of organisational efficiency. Global support is often easier to provide than allocating time to assist and observe an elderly person.
>
> ---
>
> ■**Social distance from staff**
> In hospitals conversations are mostly initiated by nurses during 'physical' care tasks and are somewhat hurried and related to the task at hand. Overall, relationships are characterised by staff dominance (principally the power to decide where, when, how and with whom elderly confused people eat, sit, sleep, bath and toilet).
>
> ---
>
> ■**Loss of individuality**
> Phrases such as 'residents', 'patients', 'patient stock' and 'the confused elderly' pervade the language. This both structures and reflects the thinking and actions of care staff.

Physical environment

Building design and living arrangements will also have a major impact on behaviour (Alexander *et al.*, 1977).

Intimacy Gradient. In a home people need a gradient of settings which have different degrees of intimacy. A bedroom is most intimate; a lounge in a group-living unit less so; a communal activity room more public still; the front entrance area most public of all. All buildings which 'house' people need a definite gradient from 'front' to 'back' from the most public spaces at the front to the most intimate spaces at the back.

Thus the layout of spaces in the building should create a sequence which begins with the entrance and the most public parts of the building, then leads into the slightly more private areas and finally to the most private domains. Each person should have a room of their own where they can retire to be alone among personal and treasured possessions and which allows families to be intimate with their loved one. This arrangement also encourages staff to regard patients and residents as individuals with a right to privacy and respect. Bathrooms and toilets should be placed between communal areas and private ones, so that elderly people can reach them comfortably from both.

Without a gradient of intimacy, behaviour is often inappropriate to context. Intimate behaviours such as toileting may take place next to a front entrance, while access to a sleeping area may be open to visitors and staff on arrival. Such a poor fit between a person and their environment can result in distressed and agitated behaviour. Living on a hospital ward can be seen as an extreme example of an 'unhealthy' person–environment fit.

Corridors. The time a resident spends between rooms can be as important as the moments spent in the rooms themselves. A corridor which is long, devoid of natural light and bare of furnishings is consistent with our worst ideas of what is meant by 'institution'.

As Alexander *et al.* describe, long corridors distort the perception of distance, interfere with verbal communication, obscure perception of the human figure and face and can generate anxiety as a result of feeling enclosed. A corridor may be considered too long when it is more than 50 feet in length. Beyond that, corridors begin to feel 'dead' and monotonous. Everything should be done to keep corridors short. They require carpets, furniture, plants, bookshelves and windows to give plenty of light.

Seating Arrangements. The conventional seating arrangement found in day centres and residential homes is typically round the wall. Such a seating design is sterile and restricts social activity. Social contact is only possible for a few people who have to shout to fellow residents sitting against the opposite wall, or who strain to turn to their neighbour. This traditional waiting-room design is not a natural arrangement for conversation. The outcome is isolated and withdrawn residents who have been effectively de-skilled socially.

It has been shown that rearranging chairs in small groups around coffee tables can almost double the level of social interaction. An attractive arrangement is a sitting circle. When people sit down to talk together they try to arrange themselves roughly in a circle. This design also encourages people to stop to talk as they walk by.

To anchor this arrangement there needs to be a natural focus. While this is often a television, this can be age-inappropriate and an unwelcome source of environmental 'noise'. There is no substitute for an artificial fire which appears alive and flickering within a lounge. Fire can be an emotional touchstone generating feelings of cosiness, homeliness and comfort. A fire attracts people to a room and makes it more likely for a group to gather.

However for an elderly resident a home is not just the lounge or bedroom, it is the building. For many, exercise and occupation will consist solely of walking around the home, and the 'nooks and crannies' to be found are all potential sitting spaces. Care staff tend to think about a 'sitting' room as if this is the only place for sitting. As human activity occurs naturally throughout the home there is a need to provide sitting spaces around the building to support the daytime rhythm of walking and 'hanging around' (Alexander *et al.*, 1977).

Other architectural and interior design features which exaggerate disability, foster dependency and undermine life quality include the following:

● Two (or multi)- storey buildings which locate living units on the top floor. Accommodated here, elderly confused residents are not only at greater risk but they are compelled to live their lives dependent on scarce staff resources for everyday pleasures away from the unit. For example, they will need to be accompanied downstairs or in the lift to enjoy a moment in the garden. The outcome tends to be few walks outside. When they do take place they tend to be communal activities, rather than a response to an individual wish.

● Non-slip shiny floors appear wet and unsafe to a pair of aged eyes. The elderly person may therefore be reluctant to embark upon a journey and thus appears apathetic, dependent and withdrawn.

● The use of pale colours. Elderly people have poor visual acuity, with particular difficulty in distinguishing these. If interior doors of bedrooms are not easy to distinguish from surrounding walls a confused person may awake and be unable to see how to get out of the room. The result is distress and heightened confusion.

• If residents are without their own furniture this emphasises the discontinuity of life following admission to an old people's home. In most instances this gives rise to insecurity and a sense of 'not belonging'. It is emotionally significant to wake up in one's own bed, see familiar objects and furnishings and thereby feel 'at home'.

Overall, the image which is conjured up by the 'ugly' word institution possesses those physical features most detrimental to quality care. With their uniform colour schemes, long, featureless corridors devoid of furnishings, high ceilings, communal living areas and lack of private space, traditional institutions are 'sick buildings'. It is difficult to imagine such places ever becoming 'homely' and inviting. In such an abnormal environment it is not surprising that unacceptable, depressed and disturbed behaviour is found, although it is true that the institution is unlikely to be entirely responsible for producing all 'problem' behaviour. The reasons for the person entering the institution in the first place may also contribute to the deviant behaviour observed.

This section has highlighted the fact that, before introducing an intervention programme, account may have to be taken of ecological issues such as institutional values, staff attitudes and building design. Stokes (1986, 1987) discusses how the wider environmental context can 'make matters worse' when dealing with challenging behaviours such as wandering and toileting difficulties.

The Ideal Institution

The inadequacies of institutional care appear endemic, but they are in fact examples of bad practice, rather than the inevitable consequence of such care. How can practice be reformed?

Objectives of care

First, there needs to be clearly defined and agreed objectives of care. These can be summarised as:

1   To respect and respond to individual need;

2   To promote life quality through the provision of personal control and choice (even if this means that people choose dependence and inactivity);

3   To provide *opportunity* for independent behaviour and age-appropriate activity that is relevant and rewarding to the individual;

4   To maintain dignity.

If these are the shared aims against which we can measure organisational performance, the means to achieve them must be well detailed.

The environmental context

Success depends upon creating an enabling environment which meets the needs of both clients and staff. Only after such a development can appropriate individual and group therapies be implemented with any prospect of lasting benefit. Necessary environmental features include the following:

Normalisation

This is the provision of a lifestyle which recognises the rights of people and maximises the 'normality' of their existence. While it is not 'normal' to live within the confines of an institution, such places exist and will continue to do so for those people suffering from severe dementia. Thus the humane requirement is to create environments which reflect normality, rather than being repositories of attitudes and practice committed to depersonalisation and dependency. Normalisation not only applies to an approach which focusses on regaining and maintaining, as far as possible, normal living patterns and valued activities relevant to each individual; it also includes the development of a domestic-style building and interior design which is as far removed as possible from the open-plan impersonal hospital ward or traditional communal residential home.

People should have available to them their own clothes, their own possessions, and to be able to have meals compatible with their preferences, to decide when they wish to go to bed and to choose what to wear. Involvement in basic domestic and household activities is consistent with expected 'normal' routines for elderly people. If people have a low level of functioning which means they can only carry out simple aspects of daily living, staff must not be patronising or talk down to them as if they are children.

Person-centred care

This requires the provision of care routines which correspond to the needs of clients. It is opposed to 'block treatment' where people are dealt with in groups. The approach to care is person-orientated rather than task-orientated. It follows therefore that regulations and rigid routines are at a minimum, for these only decrease individuality and choice.

Care does not only mean responding to physical needs; it also includes the development of acceptance, understanding and meaningful personal relationships which serve to reduce social distance. Overall, consideration is given to the 'whole' person.

A prosthetic environment

Skills and abilities which are damaged or lost are compensated for by the provision of physical and environmental prostheses. As the model of multiple pathways shows, behaviour is a function of the person and their environment, and thus, 'if behaviour is deficient, the environment could be altered in order to produce effective behaviour' (Lindsley, 1964). Prosthetic supports include grab rails, kitchen, bath and toilet facilities designed for frail and handicapped people and for those suffering from mental infirmity, memory aids, pathfinder instructions and information symbols.

The apparent conflict between normalisation and environmental prostheses is resolved through the concept of 'valued means, valued ends'. If a hierarchy of individual needs is constructed the means to achieve these valued needs are equally valued. If, for example, the aim is to encourage appropriate toileting and the means to achieve this requires directional information and symbols, then the creation of a prosthetic environment is valued. Dogmatically to follow the dictates of normalisation may result in confused people wandering around a building seeking a toilet, suffering the indignity of inappropriate urinating and soiled clothing. It has to be borne in mind that a reason for the elderly person being in institutional care is that they could not adequately function in a 'normal' environment.

Staff reward

As many professional care-givers prefer to look after dependent people and gain a sense of achievement when they successfully meet their physical needs, staff need to be encouraged and supported following a change to a regime which promotes independence and choice. Priority should be given to staff training and opportunities to broaden experience. This should take the form of a structured programme designed to meet the in-house requirements of different categories of staff. It should not be a random presentation of topics which appear interesting but have little relevance to the work needs of staff. It is important that daily work allows the trained skill to be exercised.

It is essential that senior staff are sympathetic to the needs of their junior staff, and by example and encouragement show they are 'in tune' with the new ideas being advocated. Regular staff meetings as a forum for information exchange are an example of good management practice. Staff should be free to 'speak their minds' and, regardless of their position in the organisation, enabled to feel valued and involved. And this not only applies to direct-care staff. Domestic, clerical and maintenance staff also contribute to the well-being of patients or residents and thus need to be seen as part of the 'care team'.

It cannot be denied that working in an institution for confused elderly people can be extremely stressful, and so problems of 'staff burn-out' and the need for support must not be underestimated. These and related matters are addressed in Chapter 24.

To Segregate or to Integrate, that is the Question

One of the most controversial issues in the provision of long-stay care is whether dementing elderly people should be integrated with those who are 'rational', but physically frail, or should live in segregated facilities (for example, Elderly Mentally Infirm Units).

Arguments in favour of integration

1   The frail but more able elderly act as appropriate role models for their confused peers and may also assist and support them in their daily lives. The confused elderly also benefit from the stimulation of more able residents.

2   All elderly people in residential care have the same basic needs.

3   It is wrong to deprive dementia sufferers of equal access to resources to other elderly people in long-stay care because of a 'label' of dementia.

Arguments against integration

1   Confused elderly people 'drag down' the skills level of 'rational' residents who share the same accommodation.

2   Non-dementing residents are distressed and agitated by confused people who may be noisy, disinhibited and interfere with their possessions.

3   Dementia sufferers are rejected by more able residents and thus experience a decline in life quality. Integration seldom occurs even when it is meant to happen. Confused people soon become members of an ostracised 'out-group'.

4   Although physical needs are likely to be common to both confused and rational, dementing elderly people have their own needs resulting from memory loss and intellectual deterioration.

Argument in favour of segregation

Specialist units can provide high-quality care to meet the unique needs of the dementing elderly.

Argument against segregation

Dementia sufferers are stigmatised if they are assigned to separate facilities.

Conclusion

It is the opinion of the author that the development of small specialist units designed to meet the needs of dementing elderly people in terms of providing appropriate building designs, management policy and staffing arrangements is the way to ensure good practice. Such provision may be unnecessary and an insult to intellectually able people.

Quality of life is not inevitably poorer in specialist care, nor does stigma have to be attached to such establishments. They can be seen as centres of excellence wherein dementing people can live as normal a life as their disabilities allow and be involved in valued activities and experiences. They can be the focus for community-based services supporting people in their own homes and providing respite care when necessary. Also, within such specialist units, the value, skills and commitment of staff who provide that care are more likely to be recognised.

This is not to suggest that, when a resident or patient falls below a threshold of competence, they should automatically be transferred to a specialist resource. A person who deteriorates while living in care is usually well tolerated by other residents and staff and would be distressed by the trauma of an enforced move. However, for people with severe dementia who are leaving independent arrangements, admission to specialist units which have the needs of the person as their starting-point appears to be a sympathetic and sensible policy.

Living at Home

While anonymous institutional environments are damaging, detrimental effects may arise in the familiar surroundings of a person's own home. This is a major concern, as most people suffering from dementia are not living in residential care or in hospital. It has been estimated that only 20 per cent may live in institutions. Often dementia as severe as that seen in institutions is to be found in the community.

The family home

Furnishings and layout appropriate for the needs of family life may not meet those of the aging dementia sufferer. A home located on a busy main road, steps up to the front door, a steep staircase with bedrooms and toilet located upstairs may all interfere with an elderly confused person's ability to function within the home setting. An elderly man coped with the determined wanderings of his confused wife by placing a gate at the top of the stairs at night. This minimised the risk of her falling down the stairs. Tragically, she fell from her bedroom window one night as she pursued her efforts to leave the house 'to return home' and was killed.

Problems such as leaving a gas cooker on unlit or having to cope with an open fire can place a person at particular risk. Domestic habits (for example, placing the kettle on the gas ring or hob) and routines (for example, cooking and laying the table for the family) from the past may be triggered by the familiar surroundings of the home. The consequence now is to place the person at risk or cause upset and disturbed behaviour.

Practical solutions may require replacing hazardous equipment, disconnecting or 'sabotaging' a dangerous power supply, or informing neighbours of the difficulty being experienced in order that they can become part of the support network.

The family under strain

Most families confronted with a dementing elder member care deeply about their welfare and tolerate the burden of care with remarkable fortitude. However the price paid for providing care in home surroundings can be the physical and mental exhaustion of the supporters.

When the care-giver lives with the dementia sufferer the strain of care can at times be excessive as problems mount up. The need to supervise actions as the sufferer becomes less like the person who was once known and loved can be an intolerable, unfolding tragedy. As the relationship between supporters and dependant deteriorates, a reduction in the quality of care provided is inevitable. When confused behaviour is poorly tolerated, not only is the dementia sufferer likely to react with more difficult behaviour, but supporters become aware of their own limitations and morale is consequently lowered.

Dispirited, pessimistic carers who are unable or unwilling to meet the needs of their loved one can undermine the remaining strengths of their dependants. Even more damaging is the situation when a supporter deliberately obstructs care or attempts to engineer a change in living arrangements by exaggerating dependency needs or disruptive demands. Such manipulative behaviour often happens when inadequate pre-morbid relationships make relatives reluctant to provide support. Conversely, the author worked with a loving family who were caring for their father who was suffering from MID. Yet this extremely pleasant, albeit noisy gentleman still entered long-stay psychogeriatric care, to the detriment of his welfare, because the family were unable to adjust their standards as to what was acceptable behaviour. A previously close and concerned family were consumed by embarrassment, and ultimately felt obliged to reject their father. By acting contrary to his needs they caused his behaviour to deteriorate and were able to deflect any sense of guilt at removing him from the family home by pointing to his increasingly excessive demands. The message is that secure and loving pre-morbid relationships are no guarantee that quality care will be available to meet the demands of changed circumstances. The important issues of supporting relatives and working with families are addressed in Chapter 23.

It should also be remembered that manipulation can also be practised by the dementing relative. Demanding or hypochondriacal behaviour can be used to control carers, with the unfortunate consequence that the family are less inclined to offer support. Deterioration in behaviour occurs as an increase in unreasonable demands is experienced.

The elderly person living alone

Elderly confused people living alone in their own homes are most vulnerable and thus pose significant problems. Effective supervision and management are difficult without major changes in the life-style of family supporters. The potential for risk is a great concern. A mobile, physically robust person who is unaware of their surroundings can easily get lost outside the house. Attempts to compensate for damaged skills and support remaining strengths are unlikely to be successful, given that prompting, encouragement and a watchful eye are not available within the home. Prosthetic aids (for example, memory boards, identification labels) may be removed as their use is not understood and they may be regarded as unwelcome clutter. Deficient food preparation skills can result in self-neglect, especially if 'meals on wheels' are rejected. Prescribed medication is difficult to administer, for the confused person is unlikely to remember to take the drugs, while community nurses are too thin on the ground to visit every day, let alone several times a day to give medication. Overall, the level of risk can appear unacceptable.

Although neighbours may be supportive, many, possibly because they are ignorant of what dementia means, can be critical and intolerant. Complaints to family supporters can lead to excessive worry and a blinkered view that their relative must be placed in institutional care.

In many cases, working with confused elderly people who live alone raises ethical issues of rights and responsibility. The person at risk who rejects professional advice or acts contrary to the wishes of the family should, however, still be treated as an adult with a right to live their life as they wish, despite their lack of insight and inability to exercise rational judgement. To do otherwise exposes the dementia sufferer to exploitation. Unfortunately, although understandably, such an attitude can exasperate and anger families who see this as an abrogation of professional responsibility.

Conclusion

It is clear that 'behavioural ecology' is an essential part of the process of assessment and analysis. The whole environmental context must be understood, for a failure to do so can result in only a partial appreciation of why behaviour is occurring and a subsequent failure of interventions.

A principal reason for 'working with dementia' is to slow down the rate of behavioural decline as the disease process pursues its remorseless path of cerebral devastation. And it is to environmental management and innovation that we can look to achieve this (*see Figure 9.1*). Recognition of the role of the wider environment may be the great hope for the future care of elderly people suffering from dementia. As HRH The Prince of Wales (1989) has publicly

Figure 9.1
The environment and behavioural performance

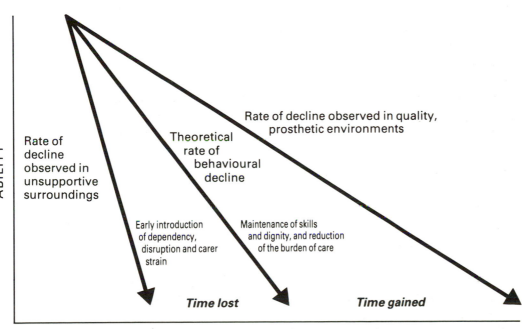

ABILITY

Rate of decline observed in unsupportive surroundings

Rate of decline observed in quality, prosthetic environments

Theoretical rate of behavioural decline

Early introduction of dependency, disruption and carer strain

Maintenance of skills and dignity, and reduction of the burden of care

Time lost

Time gained

YEARS

declared, "It is most certainly possible to design [buildings] which are positively healing … It can't be easy to be healed in a soulless concrete box with characterless windows, inhospitable corridors and purely functional wards. The spirit needs healing as well as the body."

REFERENCES

Alexander C, *A Pattern Language*, Oxford University Press, New York, 1977.
HRH The Prince of Wales, *A Vision of Britain*, Doubleday, London, 1989.
Lindsley O R, 'Geriatric Behavioural Prosthetics', R Kastenbaum (ed.), *New Thoughts On Old Age*, Springer, New York, 1964.
Stokes G, *Wandering*, Winslow Press, Bicester, 1986.
Stokes G, *Incontinence and Inappropriate Urinating*, Winslow Press, Bicester, 1987.

FURTHER READING

Gilleard C, *Living With Dementia*, Croom Helm, London, 1984.
Norman A, *Severe Dementia: The Provision of Longstay Care*, Centre for Policy on Aging, London, 1987.

Goal Planning: Towards Meeting Individual Needs

*I*nterest in individual planning (including individual programme planning, life and goal planning) and the use of key worker systems in the care and treatment of dementia sufferers have grown considerably in the last five years and follow the trends developed in the areas of mental health and mental handicap. This chapter first of all looks at the importance of individual planning and the value of identifying client or patient needs. It goes on to discuss practical ways of working out how to meet those needs, using a structured approach which builds on the individual's existing abilities, rather than attempting to 'remove problems' by reducing the person's range of activities.

Philosophy

The belief behind most forms of care planning is that individuals should be able to live a life which is of value to them. A valued life is one in which we are able to meet the needs important to us. This includes emotional and spiritual needs and the right to have as much control over our own life as possible. It takes into account more than simply having enough to eat and a roof over our heads.

Client-centred care

The purpose of individual care planning is that, where people are unable to meet their own needs, carers can work with them and, using ways which will maintain the person's dignity and respect, help them to meet important needs. This is in line with the principle of normalisation.

As already described in Chapter 9, it is particularly crucial that care staff working with dementia sufferers have a positive client-centred approach, directed at helping them to fulfil their potential. Rotating staff around units or wards and organising people to work in a task-centred way, for instance allocating to some staff the duties of helping all patients to get up, while another helps with breakfast and another bathes those who wish to have a bath, can mean that clients have a large number of people on any one day helping them with intimate personal care. The opportunity to build up a relationship with the client becomes difficult. A key worker system, where each member of staff is responsible for working closely with a small number of clients to help meet their needs, including personal care, is more appropriate and enables care staff to think of clients from the 'whole person' point of view. Furthermore, when an individual has problems remembering and recognising people, it is important that the reassurance gained from regular contact with a small number of familiar people is maintained, whether this is at home with input from home help services or in a hospital or residential home.

Assessment

The importance of careful assessment has already been identified in Chapters 6 to 9. It is essential, before working on a need or problem with someone, that careful assessment within the context of their living situation takes place.

Mrs Mathias, for instance, enjoyed making tea and toast for herself, but on a number of occasions had burnt the toast and had forgotten to fill the kettle, so that it had boiled dry. Before she and her home help embarked on a plan which might help her to continue this task, it was necessary to assess how many of the steps in the process of tea and toast making she could remember, how long her concentration span was, whether her poor eyesight might be causing a problem in establishing how much water there was in the kettle and whether anything about the layout of her kitchen and the appliances she used could be hindering her.

New glasses, and assessment and advice from a clinical psychologist and an occupational therapist, enabled the home help to work with Mrs Mathias by giving her a clear understanding of Mrs Mathias's abilities and suggesting the best way to modify some of the 'unhelpful' kitchen appliances.

Individual planning with dementia sufferers

Developing individualised plans should not be seen as a 'cure' for dementia, nor, at the other extreme, should structured approaches to maximising an individual's ability to achieve as high a quality of life as possible be rejected for dementia sufferers because they are thought to be incapable of learning or developing. It is vital that those who work with dementia sufferers understand that they *can* learn and that they *do* respond to the approaches of those who live with and care for them.

Care plans which are effective may reduce dependence on staff and free time for work on maximising strengths and enhancing self-esteem.

Developing positive plans to meet individual needs

Goal planning (Barrowclough and Fleming, 1986) provides a specific, structured approach to make the most of an elderly person's existing skills in order that their needs can be met. It is important to bear in mind, however, the 'whole life context' into which the plan should fit and the importance of altering services if important needs cannot be met within them. To this end life planning (Chamberlain, 1985) has been established as a way of identifying people's individual needs, using this information to plan and develop services to meet these needs. It is an approach which puts clients' needs first, not those of professionals or people who think they know what is best for dementia sufferers and their families. Dementia sufferers have a right to a quality of life which is as 'normal' to them as possible, whether that life is going to last for six weeks, six months or six years.

Goal Planning

The remainder of this chapter will focus on specific aspects of devising goal plans.

Establishing strengths and needs

The first stage when devising a good care plan is to identify the person's strengths and needs. Strengths include the person's abilities in all areas of day-to-day life, previous and current interests, friends and family and carers.

Strengths can be used to help and motivate the person towards tackling problems and meeting needs.

The list of strengths and needs and, indeed, the whole plan should involve the client as far as possible. If the person has problems in communicating or understanding what is being discussed, then someone close to them who is able to represent their opinion should be involved. Problems should be stated in positive terms by identifying what the person needs or needs to do, rather than dwelling on the problem as a negative issue and just describing what happens. We might say: "Mr W needs to locate the toilet and use it appropriately", instead of "Mr W keeps urinating in the fire bucket in the corridor." Although stating problems as needs in positive terms like this may seem rather long-winded, focussing on the individual in this way gives a sense of direction and indicates what could be achieved, rather than seeing the person as a collection of

Table 10.1
Mr Henry's
strengths and needs

Strengths	Needs
■Physically fit	■To be able to express his anger and frustration appropriately
■Enjoys walking around the garden and to the local shops	■To find activities which enable him to retain his fitness and interest in sport and gardening
■Interested in growing vegetables	■To take his time when he is trying to say something
■Enjoys spectator sport, particularly boxing and football	■To be able to feel more at ease with other residents
■Is cheerful when talking about sport and gardening	
■Has regular visits from his brother	

problems, such as 'incontinence' or 'dressing difficulties', which carers have to cope with.

The strengths and needs list devised between Mr Henry and his key worker is shown in Table 10.1. Mr Henry is a former builder, who used to play football for an amateur team, and who had remained physically active in his retirement. He had been admitted to a Social Services Part III home because he was having difficulty in looking after himself following the death of this wife three months previously. He was suffering from multi-infarct dementia and at times was restless and agitated to the point that he had got into a number of arguments with other residents.

Devising goal plans

One difficulty often identified by care staff when writing plans is in being precise about goals. How long- or short-term should they be? How should they be worded so that they can be understood by staff on opposite shifts or by the home helps who replace the regular ones when they go on holiday?

Realistic goal setting

1   Work on one need at a time (*see also Chapter 8*).

2   Select a need which is important to the client or patient.

3   Choose a need which has a good chance of being fulfilled in a short space of time (say four to six weeks). This means that the person is more likely to persevere because a reward is in sight. A goal plan is then devised to meet this need. Obviously some goals will only be fulfilled over much longer periods, but they should be broken down into small steps which can be fulfilled more quickly. For those with a very impaired memory, steps will need to be small enough to be achieved after a few minutes.

4   Goal plans devised to meet needs should always be written positively (*see figure 10.1*). A good goal plan will state:
    a)   *What* the individual will be doing when the goal is achieved;
    b)   *Who* they will do it with;
    c)   *How* they will do it;
    d)   *When* they will do it.

The figure below shows Mr Henry's goal.

Figure 10.1
Mr Henry's goal

Client's Name: Mr Henry	Date: 19 July 1990

Present Behaviour
Mr Henry currently gets restless and agitated in Wisteria House, to the extent that he takes his frustration out on other residents. He complains that 'he isn't doing enough these days, and doesn't know anyone in the home'. He gets lost when he goes out alone, so requires someone to accompany him.

Need Selected (from Table 10.1)
Mr Henry needs to find activities which enable him to retain his fitness and interest in sport and gardening.

Goal
Mr Henry will go each fortnight to the football match played at the local sports ground with Mr Wilson (who lives at Wisteria House and also enjoys football) and his brother Fred, who visits on Saturdays.

Steps to achieving the goal
Step 1: Mr Henry will go on a short walk in the gardens of Wisteria House with Fred on his weekly visits.

Step 2: Mr Henry will go for a walk to the park with Fred each Saturday.

Step 3: Mr Henry will go to the town shopping centre on alternate Saturday afternoons with Fred and Mr Wilson.

Step 4 (Goal): Mr Henry will go each fortnight to the local league football match with Fred and Mr Wilson.

5   Each small step is a mini-goal (*see Figure 10.1*) which enables the individual to work towards the main goal gradually. The amount of work required for each step will depend on how quickly the client is able to learn new things and how much time the carer is able to spend working with them. It is important to establish a measure of success for each small step so that it is clear to everyone that the client is ready to move on to the next. For instance, Mr Henry began to go on short walks with his brother, which he

enjoyed, gradually building up to going to a football match. It was important to build up to this gradually as his confidence had been eroded by his disabilities and he could have become very agitated going to 'the match' and having to cope with the crowds and the need to concentrate. Seeing how he coped with increasingly longer trips out meant that everybody, including Mr Henry, was confident he would enjoy the outing. The achievement of this goal in the company of Mr Wilson helped Mr Henry meet another need — that of feeling more at ease with other residents.

6   Think of how a client's strengths may help in meeting needs. Note how Mr Henry's interest in football was used in his general plan.

Evaluation

Evaluate a client's progress regularly and modify the plan if necessary. This is essential if plans are to be active processes leading to change and not pieces of paper stored in a file which never see daylight because client and carer alike feel that nothing is being achieved. Sometimes over-ambitious goals are set and need to be modified. People with dementia will deteriorate over time and the plan may aim at reducing the rate of deterioration, rather than making a dramatic improvement. Thus it is important to acknowledge that not everyone is going to be able to carry out tasks independently. For instance, Mrs Arrowsmith needed maximum help from her husband with dressing. An identified need was that she should be helped to select her clothes from a choice of two or three garments, to enable her to retain some control of *what* she wore.

Abstract needs

Although the above points are most helpful when dealing with observable behaviours, it is equally important to have a structure for more abstract issues; otherwise statements like: 'Needs to be at peace with himself' or 'Needs to make more choices in her life' will remain as ideals written in files rather than being translated into positive changes in the lives of individuals.

Conclusion

Goal planning encourages staff to adopt a client-centred attitude where people's past interests and existing abilities are maintained and used to help them cope with needs and problems. The idea of identifying strengths and needs seems to encourage staff to think positively about clients and to develop favourable attitudes towards them. Timetabling when actions are to be carried out, scheduling meetings to discuss an issue and deciding areas of responsibility can all be of help in goal planning. Little work has been done on involving the families of dementia sufferers in goal planning. However, where this has been successful, relatives are involved early on and their needs are also taken into account.

REFERENCES

Barrowclough C and Fleming I, *Goal Planning with Elderly People. Making Plans to Meet Individual Needs. A Manual of Instruction*, Manchester University Press, 1986.

Chamberlain P, *Life Planning Manual*, British Association of Behavioural Psychotherapy, Rossendale, 1985.

Fiona Goudie, Rosemary Bennett &
Anita Steed

CHAPTER 11

The Maintenance of Independence

*I*t is important that people with dementia are encouraged to do as much for themselves as possible, for as long as possible, in order to retain skills, maintain a sense of usefulness and thereby preserve self-esteem. Success is important, particularly in the early stages of dementia, when the person still has insight into their difficulties. In many ways confidence re-building is the first step in encouraging independent behaviour. Therefore activities and tasks should be realistic and achievable. Retained abilities must be highlighted.

Chapter 10 discussed ways to devise structured plans to help people meet particular needs. This chapter identifies the specific ways in which carers can encourage and maintain skills in daily living activities.

General Guidelines

1 An individualised daily routine is a good idea, perhaps written into a diary or onto a calendar. Carers need to appreciate the importance of predictable, regular routines as a means by which the dementing person can achieve a degree of control over the uncertainties of daily life.

2 The carer should know the person's preferred 'order' for carrying out a daily routine or specific task. Too often care plans talk about putting clothes on or washing in the 'correct' order or sequence, without

specifying what the correct order is for the individual. Think about your own pattern of dressing, bathing or using the toilet. Do you think it is likely that an unfamiliar person would be able to predict your habits? It is vital that individuals and relatives are involved in providing professionals with this information.

3   The person should be encouraged to carry out the steps they can do on their own. If an excess of help is provided the unfortunate consequence is likely to be a de-skilled, de-motivated dementia sufferer.

4   Where a person has difficulty with a 'step' such as pulling pants down or using a knife to cut meat, a hierarchy of help should be constructed. This goes from least to most help. Only if the person cannot 'do it for themselves' is more help provided by progressing through the hierarchy.

   a)   Verbally describe what the person needs to do and prompt as they go along. 'Talking through' can be helpful for those with recognition problems.

   b)   If the person has comprehension problems, use mime or gesture to show what they need to do.

   c)   Describe and mime what the person needs to do.

   d)   Start the person off on the task (eg. help put their feet into their trousers) but encourage them to finish the task themselves, using step (a), (b) or (c), whichever seems most useful.

   e)   If the person needs a great deal of help, try to encourage them to help do the very last part of it, such as straightening clothes, drying face after body has been dried. This gives the individual a sense of having completed something for themselves. This method is known as backward chaining. Concentrating on the skills closest to completion motivates relearning. Once acquired, preceding skills can be learned with the knowledge that the chain can be completed. This once again serves to encourage the relearning of dormant skills.

5   Praise should be used when the person has succeeded, but this should not be overdone. A simple 'fine', 'good' or 'well done' is enough. Remember you are working with an adult who has carried out the task independently in the past, not a child who is doing it for the first time.

6   It can be useful to initially praise attempts which approximate the target

skill. So long as the person performs the behaviour reasonably, they can be praised and encouraged. After several attempts, the standard required can be made more precise, so that praise is forthcoming only when the target is more accurately achieved. This process is known as 'shaping'.

7   The 'prompt–praise' approach will not work for everyone. In particular people with apraxia (*see Chapter 6*) may be better left alone to try to find their own 'spontaneous' solution, rather than the carer trying to help them by describing or demonstrating the skill. Direct instruction will only interfere with the chances of success.

Special neuropsychological rehabilitation strategies to help with problems such as apraxia are described in the next chapter.

8   Rehearsal and practice of a particular step in a task may be helpful. Although dementia is an insidious process and new skills are often not retained for long, frequent practice can sometimes be of help, particularly in the earlier stages of the disease.

9   If the above ideas do not help the person to employ normal tools for a task, the use of special appliances (for example, cups, cutlery) is advised. Overall, the likelihood of skills being maintained is increased if the obstacles between the person and independent behaviour are minimised. Such action may involve the introduction of building prosthetics (for example, grab rails), clothing adaptations and 'safe' household equipment. However suggestions must be realistic. There is no point suggesting to a partner with a state retirement pension as their only means of support that they consider major building renovations or purchase expensive equipment!

The following are examples of basic environmental prostheses which help promote independent or assisted action.

a)   Provide information by using:

- clear labels and signs to identify tins, packets and rooms; when appropriate use words and pictures.
- colour coding of doors, symbols and directional information, so that, for example, all water-related activities such as toileting and bathing are colour-coded blue (*see Chapter 13*).
- notice boards which are regularly up-dated and used for reference.

●accurate clocks.

●calendars.

●diaries and notebooks; these should be used and not left forgotten in a drawer.

●appropriate other clues, for example, posters relevant to time of year; newspapers.

●staff name badges; these should not be simply worn, but staff should also point out who they are.

b)   Meet safety needs by introducing:

●rails by bath, stairs, corridors, toilets.

●appropriate heating and cooking equipment that can be used safely; gas fires may need to be replaced by storage heaters; an extra gas tap can be fixed behind a gas cooker which can ensure gas supply is turned off, unless a carer is in the house.

●key boards. A person with dementia living alone should be encouraged to keep door keys in a prominent place. A set of keys tied inside a handbag can also be useful in ensuring a person does not lock themselves out.

●bright lighting, particularly in corridors and toilets. However avoid lights that cause or cast shadows.

10   Overall, it is essential that carers are consistent in their approach to the confused person. All supporters need to be familiar with the aims and objectives of the structured plans. If there is an absence of continuity, staff will make differing demands on the dementia sufferer and, as a result, promote uncertainty and dependence.

The rest of this chapter explores problems which may occur in specific areas of skill and provides ideas which may be incorporated to help make the most of the individual's abilities and compensate for difficulties.

Communication

It is often a good idea to use a light touch, perhaps on the arm, when communicating, because it can have a reassuring effect, conveying empathy and warmth. Clear speech and eye contact are equally important when communicating. Do avoid speaking with a hand over the mouth or with head turned.

For those with aphasia (*see Chapter 6*) it is helpful to use visual clues. Pointing to a picture of a toilet when asking if the person needs to use it may aid comprehension. It is easy to distract the confused person by saying too many things in one go. Pace what you say, use simple sentences and try to get one idea across at a time.

Avoid talking over the head of the individual to relatives and carers; this is degrading and can cause bewilderment. Include the confused person in these conversations and repeat yourself if necessary. Remember that the reply may be delayed, so be prepared to wait. If the individual has difficulty with expression, try to observe eyes, hands and intonation, to see if these help convey what they are trying to say. (*For further advice on communication difficulties, see Chapter 15.*)

Self-care

Washing and shaving

Lay out the flannel, soap and towel, etc so that they are in the individual's preferred order of use. If a man uses an electric razor make sure he does so away from water.

Bathing

Independent bathing is often an early skill to be lost; the person forgets to bathe or becomes frightened. Self-bathing can be broken into broad component parts, such as undressing, getting into the bath, soaping, rinsing, getting out of the bath, drying and dressing. Supervision by a carer or bath attendant is advisable; the level of supervision will depend on the degree of cognitive impairment and physical disability. The depth of water should be reduced so that the person feels safe. To increase safety, appropriate equipment can be provided, such as a shower, bath board, seat, non-slip mat and grab rails.

Toileting

During the daytime encourage the individual to go to the toilet regularly. You should have an idea of their usual frequency of using the toilet and remind them that the appropriate interval has passed (*see Chapter 18*). If the toilet is passed during the course of the day, encourage them to take the opportunity to use it. To help the confused person during the night, leave the toilet light on with the door open. If mobility is a problem, or the toilet is outside, it may be wise to leave a commode by the bed. But remember that, for most people, using the lavatory is the more desirable option if this can be achieved.

For people with toileting difficulties which are not improved by prompting or environmental modification, the following ideas may help avoid embarrassment. Protect the bed with plastic sheets and a draw sheet – an ordinary sheet folded in half. This may prevent having to change the entire bed in the middle of the night. However the attitude of carers should not be one of 'we have now given permission for you to wet the bed'. Disposable pants and pads can be used, but beware of insulting the individual's dignity by asking them to use them. They can easily be seen as degrading.

Dressing

Verbal or visual prompts may be necessary to maintain levels of independence. The continued use of familiar items of clothing is advisable. The identification of dressing apraxia during assessment will need particular help (*see Chapter 12*). Any physical difficulties, as with reaching feet to put stockings on or doing up buttons, may be rectified by the use of small aids. However the ability to learn how to use a new piece of equipment will require practice and may be limited. Slip-on shoes, front fastenings for dresses and velcro in place of buttons or zippers can make dressing easier. Materials which are easily washable and retain their shape are recommended.

Some people with dementia may not want to be helped to get dressed, even though this is necessary. It is then advisable to divert the person's attention and be relaxed in approach and attitude.

Meal Times

It is important to retain the individual's dignity and self-respect at meal times. As far as possible use ordinary cutlery and crockery. Some cutlery has thick handles and ordinary plates with rims can help avoid spillage. The use of napkins to minimise the burden of deteriorating eating skills is 'normal' and thus more readily accepted by a dementia sufferer.

Present only one course at a time, and one set of utensils. If assistance with eating is indicated, cut the food into bite-size pieces, but only do this if the person cannot do it for themselves with appropriate prompts.

Special plates, cutlery and cups may help, if they make the difference between someone eating on their own rather than being helped to do so. Dycem matting can be useful to help prevent the plate moving, and a plate guard can prevent food being pushed off the plate. Tea-time can be made easier by making it a 'finger buffet'.

Household Activities

Encourage the confused person to take part in simple tasks — making the bed, vacuuming, dusting, washing up, drying up, making the tea, peeling vegetables. Think of activities which may be useful — gardening, window cleaning, sweeping the path.

Shopping and budgeting

These are complex activities. Most people with dementia will require help from the early stages. A particular problem is buying inappropriate items or hoarding large quantities of certain items, which will be denied. It is often local tradespeople who bring this to the attention of a partner or other family members. Including a relative or, for example, a home help in shopping trips to assist in selecting and purchasing items will help minimise this problem.

Tea-making

This is often a well learnt skill and therefore maintained for a longer period. This should be encouraged, with or without supervision, using familiar equipment. Monitoring of this skill is important to ensure safety as abilities gradually decline.

Meal preparation

This is a complex activity, from planning to serving up. Most identified problems are sequencing difficulties, due, for example, to poor short-term memory, apraxia or perseveration (*see Chapter 6*). If any of these difficulties have been identified, the person should only be encouraged to continue preparing meals so long as support is available for the parts that are beyond remaining skills. A sense of usefulness can be maintained by the carer ensuring that only achievable tasks, such as peeling potatoes and washing up, are undertaken. In all instances patience and acceptance are necessary on the part of the carer.

Laundry

Encouragement of simple hand washing (of tights and pants for instance) should be maintained as long as possible.

Conclusion

While attempts to help confused people maintain their independence may be time-consuming and, at times, frustrating, it is worthwhile persevering. Working on increasing and maintaining self-care skills not only encourages a dementing person to feel useful and helps them hold onto their self-respect, but in the long run it reduces the excessive burden of care which arises when people with *some* dependency needs are de-skilled and becoming increasingly unable or unwilling to practise self-care behaviour. Time spent now monitoring and assisting people with personal care tasks can save scarce and valuable time later.

Neuropsychological Deficits: Rehabilitation & Retraining

*N*europsychology is not only concerned with identifying the nature of brain–behaviour relationships and disorder, it also focusses on the issues of rehabilitation and retraining. Many problems can be managed by considering commonsense approaches to the challenging behaviour. Rehabilitation sessions should be short, frequent and interesting to the client, with plenty of praise and encouragement.

Aphasias*

When managing the difficulty of speech disorder it is essential to use simple sentences, speak slowly, give time and remember that gesture, tone and melody are the concern of other brain systems and can be understood (*see Chapter 15 for more on this*).

Apraxias

Avoid direct instructions, encourage automatic responses and dilute attention to a task by chatting or asking the person to hum or sing while performing it. Distraction is the important element of retraining apraxic individuals. A series of

*See Chapter 6 for definition of this and other terms used in this chapter.

pictures with step-by-step instructions on how to shave or how to make a sandwich can help an apraxic person complete a task. This exercise splits concentration between performing the actions and following the instructions. Demonstrating with actual objects can also help.

Dressing apraxia may be improved by:

- *Colour*: red tabs on the back of clothes; a yellow tab with 'left' for the left shoe, and a green tab with 'right' for the right shoe;
- *Order*: lay out clothes in the order in which that particular individual usually dresses;
- *Assistance*: mime what to do, or start the person off.

Aims should be low at first, allowing the person to do as much alone as possible, giving lots of time and working step by step. Overall, guidance depends on the person's needs and difficulties.

Agnosias

Allow the person to use other senses as well as the obvious one for recognition of an object. Using touch, taste and smell as appropriate, in addition to sight, will hasten normal identification.

Anosognosia can be helped by commonsense strategies. Turn the plate around when the person finishes eating the food on the side within their vision. Talk and work with the client from the side of which they are aware. Encourage awareness of the neglected side by moving slowly into it, so as to widen the range of attention.

Prosopagnosia is hard to treat. Matching the sound of familiar voices with photographs of 'forgotten' faces can be a help.

Frontal Lobe Damage

Perseveration is probably most successfully managed by abrupt distraction. As the irritating phrase, sentence or word begins, some form of distraction should be initiated. A question may be useful. Other occasions might require a loud handclap or similar action to startle the person sufficiently to interrupt the repetition. As soon as attention is caught, and the perseveration ceases, time should be spent talking to the person pleasantly.

With repeated gesture or movements, it is necessary to interrupt the action with a gentle, restraining hand. This should be done just as the gesture commences.

Poor sequencing ability may benefit from staged practice in ordering things. Breaking down a task into its component parts and drawing the person's attention to each separate part is one strategy. Simple, sequential pictures or picture stories can be useful. An exercise might be to ask the client to sort pictures of, for example, spring, summer, autumn and winter, or baby, child and adult into the correct order.

Conclusion

Though the above suggestions are only a starting point, it is hoped that they go some way towards helping carers respond to the challenge of providing answers or programmes to overcome or alleviate neuropsychological disorders.

FURTHER READING

Holden U P (ed.), *Neuropsychology and Aging*, Croom Helm, London, 1988.

Reality Orientation in the 1990s

*T*he development of reality orientation (RO) can be traced back to the early 1960s, when James Folsom in the United States introduced the practice for elderly patients. However it is likely that similar therapeutic work was already being used in psychiatric rehabilitation programmes.

RO is essentially a means of helping people to remember, hold onto their skills, abilities and experiences, to relearn some skills, express their personalities and enjoy their lives as much as possible. Carers assist by ensuring that the necessary support, opportunities, materials and attitudes are available, and that the environment is modified to suit the client, rather than the other way around.

What is RO?

Originally, in the United States, 'classroom RO' implied formal group sessions stressing the repetition of name, day, date and weather. Some sort of information board was used as a focus. Other 'classroom' activity would also use a focus, such as a piece of music or a picture to help the group members to contribute to, and retain information about, a common topic under discussion.

The first controlled study came from the United Kingdom in 1975, when Brook, Degun and Mather demonstrated significant improvements in the verbal orientation of dementia sufferers who had participated in formal RO when compared to those who had not. Literature reviews and practical information on RO are outlined in Holden and Woods (1988).

Informal or 24-hour RO was designed to help people to appreciate their whereabouts and the events around them. Carers present accurate information in everyday conversation and provide a commentary on what is happening as they engage with the dementing person. Confused, rambling speech is corrected or ignored. RO is ideally a 24-hour process, with formal or 'classroom' RO an intensive form to supplement the 'informal' approach.

As we enter the 1990s, the use of RO in a wider sense is firmly advocated. It is not simply the practice of reminding people of the day, date, place and the names of those around them. It is ethically unsound to orientate somebody towards a reality if the quality of the 'here and now' is harsh and unrewarding. Reality can be disordered if people in contact with elderly confused people do not behave in a 'normal' manner. Just because a person lives in a hospital or residential home, it does not follow that social courtesy is forgotten, that past status is ignored or that those providing a service, such as hairdressers or shopkeepers, no longer need to treat the elderly customer in the same way as any other customer. RO is a good way of promoting positive staff attitudes to help people live as normally as possible. By helping people to remain in touch with the here and now a level of reasonable independence is encouraged.

Formal RO

A small group (five to six clients) is led by two therapists in a private area with a good social atmosphere. Settings can vary from a simulated bar to a cosy, comfortable area which is quiet and private. Table 13.1 identifies the essential ingredients of formal RO. Today this format remains common, but individual goals are now often included and a wide range of activities, such as reminiscence, exercise, and games, are featured within which RO principles can be practised.

24-hour RO

RO is a means of reducing confusion, minimising excess disabilities and promoting independent action. Obviously this is a 24-hour process. Errors in care practice can sometimes limit or prevent the practice of effective RO. These errors are summarised in Table 13.2.

Table 13.1
The essentials of
formal RO

- Group members are of similar abilities and hold similar interests.
- Stimulating materials are provided to aid concentration.
- The atmosphere is non-threatening, eg. answers are gently provided when response is incorrect.
- Programmes are planned, recorded and monitored.
- Individual strengths and needs are emphasised.
- Aims or goals are simple — a step at a time.
- Repetition is important; names and references to what is happening are mentioned frequently in as many different ways as possible.
- Boredom leading to reversals is avoided by keeping pace with improvements.
- Basic, standard and advanced grouping is used as appropriate.
- Reinforcement and encouragement are constantly in use.

Table 13.2
Possible errors

- Many clients, despite age and infirmity, are intelligent, cultured and experienced — this can be overlooked.
- Everyone needs choice, control of their lives (within reason) and support rather than interference.
- Deprivation of normal routine, sensory input and stimulation equals 'brain-washing'.
- Communication can be impaired by forgetting to employ touch, eye contact and explanation as appropriate.
- Humiliating and odd behaviour by 'supporters' is damaging; eg. a barber who shaves an elderly man without first consulting him about how or whether it should be done is hardly reality-oriented!

RO into the 1990s

Figure 13.1 represents the developments that have occurred in RO since the 1960s. Errors still happen; RO limited to day, date, names and weather invites boredom and limits the opportunity for success. Reality consists of much more

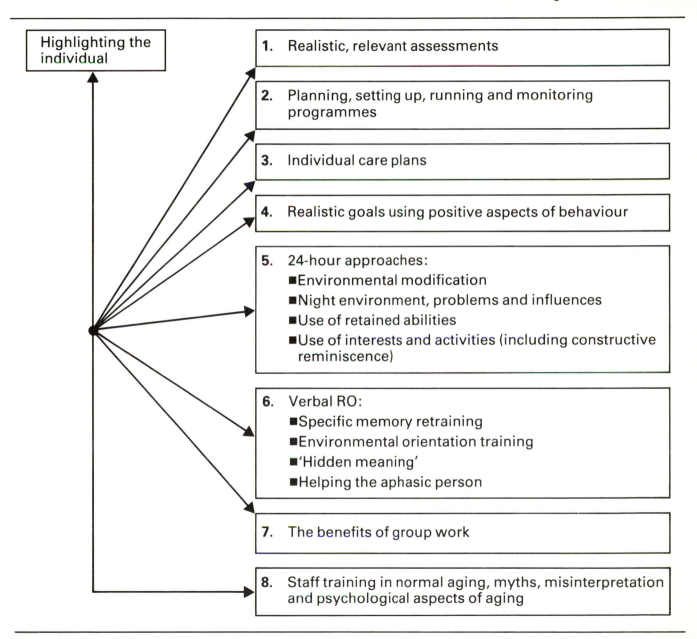

Figure 13.1 RO into the 1990s

than temporal orientation, which in any case is not a problem restricted to dementia sufferers since mistakes about time can be made by people of all ages. Time is important, but so are people, places, events and abilities. Today the stress is on the individual and that person's strengths and needs.

Realistic and relevant assessment

The more that is known about a person, the more 'tools' are available. Many test procedures useful with healthy, able people are not appropriate for the frail and confused. Tests should be undemanding, brief and not stressful. As much information as possible should be obtained from observation of everyday activity, from conversation and from discussions with relatives.

Setting up, running and monitoring a programme

Frequently the enthusiasm to help overrides common sense. Careful planning is essential. Details such as planning rotas, allowing for sick leave and holidays, choosing equipment, finding space and gaining familiarity with the method to be used all take time and thought. Sabotage can come from many sources and is often self-inflicted, owing to impatience. Useful guidelines on running a successful RO programme are featured in Table 13.3.

Table 13.3
Features of a
successful RO
programme

There should be:
■Working partners on good terms
■Notes and records
■Regular support and discussion sessions for staff
■A set period of time in which to run the programme
■Regular evaluations to indicate the need for change or modification
■A break during which further developments can be planned

Individual care plans

These make use of goal and life planning, strengths and needs. Retraining of memory, improving hygiene, working on speech problems and social difficulties can make use of RO principles on a one-to-one basis. More on individual planning can be found in Chapter 10.

Mrs Penny was a great organiser and excellent cook before her husband died. Then came confusion and disarray. The Day Hospital's step-by-step plan encouraged her to try to be her old self. So in the first week she successfully made tea for the RO group and the following week she prepared a lunch. Later she helped staff to plan events.

Realistic goals using positive aspects of behaviour

Any goal must be *realistic*. If the problem is a severe speech defect the return of normal speech is an unrealistic aim; improved communication would be more appropriate. Each small step leads to a larger one.

Mrs Brown's minor stroke left her with weak left fingers and depression made her unco-operative with physiotherapy. She had previously loved music and believed that she would never play the piano again. On the rehabilitation unit a miniature piano was found and she was persuaded to play it with her left hand. Everyone applauded. After an hour she complained and asked to use the hospital piano; within another hour she asked to be discharged as her own piano had been properly tuned! Within a few days finger strength improved.

24-hour approaches

Environmental modification

The environment plays a major role in our lives and influences the well-being of those in care. (*See Chapter 9.*) Any of us can become confused by a strange place and yet an old person who has lived independently for the past 50 years is often expected to adapt quickly to a residential setting. The number of strange faces encountered each day is confusing enough but there are added problems remembering the whereabouts of toilets, rooms and beds. Common sense dictates the need to use colour, notices and a personal guide to assist learning.

The home needs to be well-lit, floors should look safe and even, and information should be easy to find and see.

Night-time

Too frequently the hours between 7 pm and 7 am are forgotten, yet these hours are most significantly associated with heightened disorientation and confused behaviour. Night staff obtain minimal training and have little say in care planning or interventions. Clients' needs are also forgotten. Generally the evening is regarded as the time to relax, to be entertained or to socialise, eventually to retire to a personal bedroom. In an institutional setting, particularly in hospital, such activity and privacy are lost. Evenings are boring and encourage cat-napping, usually ending in a disturbed night. On wards, bed areas are public, noisy and demeaning. Staff suffer from a lack of updated information, poor understanding of the nature of sleep and inadequate awareness of relearning programmes, and have limited contact with other professionals (*see Table 13.4*). Often the lack of clean sheets and extra blankets and limited space around beds add to their difficulties. Screening around beds may be lacking or there is a tendency to use public toileting or washing. Even if a client's privacy is invaded only once in a while their status as human beings is eroded.

Night conditions play a major role — for good or ill — in rehabilitation. There is an urgent need for *24-hour* observations and better understanding of sleep and nocturia (night-time urgency or frequency of micturition).

Table 13.4 Needs of night staff	■Improved working conditions and equipment at night ■Special training regarding night influences ■The use of environmental assessments of conditions at night ■Improved contact and involvement between day and night staff ■Specialist supervisor to aid and advise at night ■Insight into the 24-hour day ■Help to make evenings more in keeping with normal living patterns, individualised for each client

Mrs Beryl Phillips, who was normally independent and socially active, was admitted for a minor complaint. She found herself sharing a bedroom with strangers who were often noisy and confused. The toilet was not nearby and there were no screens, so public toileting and washing were commonplace. She was too anxious and shy to protest and unable to sleep at night. She tried to rest during the day, thus disturbing her normal routine. She became sleepy and confused and dementia was thought to be the cause.

This 'diagnosis' of 'dementia' sounds overdramatic, but it does occur and only a 24-hour assessment can help clarify the problem. Here RO is concerned with providing normal human conditions, recognising individual dignity, privacy and normal routine. It also recognises that staff conditions, morale and training will affect the 'good' practice of RO.

Retained abilities

Despite apparent deterioration there are usually retained abilities. Frequently these are not identified and only problems are noted. In focussing on positive factors attitudes can effectively be changed. (The importance of emphasising strengths is expanded in Chapter 10.)

Using interests and activities

If staff think about their own daily activities they can identify a variable pattern. Having a cup of tea while reading the paper is as much an activity as building a house: it is just different and meets different needs. Elderly people also need variation in daily activity.

In 24-hour RO, activities will vary from hour to hour and from individual to individual. The wide range of activities is endless and depends on staff imagination and inventiveness. (*See Chapter 16 for more on activity and stimulation.*) Reminiscence, of a constructive nature, is particularly valuable. Happy memories, shared experiences and the opportunity to inform others opens up doors, develops relationships and enhances social behaviour (*see Chapter 14*).

Verbal RO

Specific memory retraining

Specific memory training now focusses on particular difficulties — remembering appointments, an anniversary, the whereabouts of the toilet and so on. Simple reminders, regular retraining sessions using diaries, photographs, physical direction and guidance, visual aids and step-by-step aims are the usual methods employed. The client's concerns should always be considered.

Environmental orientation training

Environmental orientation is valuable. Often, when directed which way to go by another person, the learner follows blindly, only to get lost when the guide is not present. With a new resident it is easy enough to point out the way but it is important for the guide eventually to stand back, ask the person to be escort, provide prompts and continue the process until learning is complete. This may involve daily practice with a key worker.

'Hidden meaning'

Many remarks made by elderly people have a hidden meaning. We all know the lady who says 'I must go and make Mum's tea' or the person who wants to go to work. Staff spend hours explaining Mum's death or retirement years ago, all to no avail. Confrontations are rarely successful or worthwhile, and often there is a reason, other than organic damage, for the remarks. It is common sense to try to understand the messages that are behind such statements made by confused people: the situation could be boring or threatening and the person wishes to escape; the person may wish to establish status and be recognised and esteemed; they may wish to be back in the past with people who were close and caring.

Distraction can be a response, or giving the person an opportunity to talk about the past may be appropriate. "It must have been nice when your mother was there; what did you have for tea?" could be one reply, or "That's right, I forgot, you used to own a restaurant, didn't you Mr Lee?" would give Mr Lee the chance to establish status. In both these replies the past tense is used with care, recognising the person's feelings and yet correcting the time perspective. In due course the person will probably use the past tense too, though at first it might be resented. This approach is known as 'time-shift'.

Helping the aphasic person

Clients may have residual communication deficits after a stroke and speech output or understanding may be limited. Gesture or pictorial material will prove useful, and slower speech, simple sentences and time to assimilate and respond should be the rule.

The benefits of group work

Formal RO can extend and reinforce most of the benefits of 24-hour RO. Groups and group identity are vital to most of us and when isolated from them we become vulnerable and uneasy. In institutional settings elderly people are deprived of a group identity and exposed to an often hierarchical and rigid organisation. This can be frightening. Staff should be responsible for creating client groups such as Formal RO in order to assist the growth of group identity and security. Feeling wanted, esteemed and able to contribute can have remarkable effects on confused old people.

Training

To expect staff to perform miracles with frail, confused people without specialist knowledge and skills is unreasonable. Once hope for improvement was viewed with scepticism, myths were rampant and diagnosis was vague. Increased knowledge, innumerable examples of change, the discovery of reversible dementias and the growing awareness of psychological factors, together with the development of new skills, have led to an improved service. All this has also put tremendous responsibilities onto the shoulders of training officers, who play a vital role in influencing attitudes and practice.

For families, relative support groups, voluntary organisations and professional staff are the main sources of information. They can help relatives appreciate the benefits of RO and provide them with simple guidelines on how to practise the techniques at home.

Conclusion

Developments in Reality Orientation go beyond the traditional RO Group with its focus on orientating people in time, place and person. In the 1990s RO will be a 24-hour approach, emphasising positive aspects of the individual's behaviour which uses strengths to meet needs in the areas of orientation and day-to-day memory. Staff will need to be up to date with the latest methods of memory retraining so that they can incorporate this into their own care practice and pass skills on to relatives.

REFERENCES

Brooke P, Degun G and Mather M, 'Reality Orientation, a Therapy for Psychogeriatric Patients: A Controlled Study', *British Journal of Psychiatry* 127 pp 42–5, 1975.

Holden U P and Woods R T, *Reality Orientation: Psychological Approaches to the 'Confused' Elderly* (2nd edn) Churchill Livingstone, Edinburgh, 1988.

FURTHER READING

Bender M, Norris A and Bauckham P, *Group Work With the Elderly*, Winslow Press, Bicester, 1987.

Hanley I, *Individualised Reality Orientation*, Dumfries, 1988.

Holden U P, *RO Reminders*, Winslow Press, Bicester, 1984.

Holden U P, *Thinking it Through*, Winslow Press, Bicester, 1984.

Reminiscence with Dementia Sufferers

*R*eminiscence, which can be defined as the process of recalling past events or experiences, features extensively in the activities of day centres, hospitals and residential homes for elderly people. Reminiscence 'therapy' is often thought to consist of encouraging people to recall in groups the pleasant memories associated with a particular era. Thoughts are triggered by the use of pictures, slide–tape shows (the *Recall Package* available from Age Concern is one example) and group members are encouraged to talk about these.

However reminiscence is not a uniform process with everyone in a particular group being equally stimulated or motivated to talk about pleasant recollections of life in the 1920s or 1940s. This chapter will look at some of the theories which exist about the function of reminiscence and will go on to consider ways in which it can be useful in working with dementia sufferers. Dementing elderly people have at times been excluded from reminiscence sessions as reminiscence has been considered to be an activity which requires a good long-term memory and the ability to talk about these memories to a group of other people. However carefully structuring the activity to take account of the individual and their memory and communication difficulties can enable dementing people to benefit from reminiscence.

Reminiscence as an Activity for Older People

Until the 1960s, those working with older people saw reminiscence as a harmful activity. It was thought that it could create misery and depression. Staff were encouraged to divert the attention of patients and clients into games and activities in the here and now, like bingo and sing-songs, rather than allow them to dwell on the past. However, in 1963, a psychiatrist called Robert Butler wrote a paper on the importance to the individual of reviewing their life in order to come to terms with their life events and experiences. He called this process 'life review'. Life review is a more in-depth procedure than that offered by reminiscence and requires a skilled counsellor or therapist, but, none the less, since Butler wrote this paper, recalling past experiences has been seen as a beneficial activity for elderly people.

Reminiscence may help to serve a variety of psychological needs. It can help preserve self-respect, encourage people to value their lives and achievements and it encourages other people to view these positively too. As stories from the past are recounted, elderly people can 'become' again what they once were. It also enables an elderly person to highlight their uniqueness at a time when individuality is poorly respected. Finally, it can, for a moment, change dominance relationships, for clients can talk about subjects *they* know more about.

It is important to remember that reminiscence is something that happens at all ages — particularly when we are going through change, such as moving house or changing jobs — it is not only a pastime of older people. Individuals differ in the extent to which they reminisce. Reminiscing is positive for many people but there are plenty of well-adjusted people who do not reminisce because they are more interested in the present or future. There are those who may feel bad about past experiences and go over and over them, 'compulsively reminiscing' but finding no real relief in the activity. There are also people who block out all recollection of the past because it is too painful to cope with the feeling it arouses. Peter Coleman (1986) discusses these differences in reminiscence style in detail. As with all interventions you cannot prescribe reminiscence, for the needs of the individual must remain paramount. For some people reminiscence is helpful and enjoyable, for others it may be a pastime to be shunned.

Who should be Involved in Reminiscence?

It is vital to bear in mind an individual's previous interest in reminiscence. Before involving them in group or individual exercises they or someone who knows them well should be asked about whether they enjoyed talking or remembering particular events and what these were, whether they seemed to get upset over certain topics or whether they preferred not to talk about the past at all.

As mentioned earlier, it has been the practice in some settings to exclude people with memory impairments from reminiscence sessions. However dementia sufferers can benefit greatly from well structured sessions which take their difficulties into account. People with mild impairments become more animated and talkative amongst themselves and with staff if they are able to talk about something which they know a good deal about. Strengths can be maximised as remote memory is less affected than recent memory in the early stages of dementia.

People with more severe difficulties should not be excluded just because they cannot talk about their reminiscences. Objects and items which trigger as many senses as possible should be available. An individual recollection does not have to be shared with everyone else to be valuable. Mrs Donovan, for instance, seemed to take very little interest in the theatre group who were leading a reminiscence session at the day centre she attended. She wandered in and out of the room throughout the afternoon, stopping for only a few minutes when encouraged to throw confetti at the couple dressed in wedding attire. Later her husband reported that she had been less restless at home that evening and had been humming 'The Wedding March'.

For many of us, reminiscence is a personal experience and we do not have to verbalise our thoughts to benefit from it.

Running Reminiscence Activities

Individual reminiscence profiles (IRPs)

It is important to know everyone's date of birth and dates of key events in their lives such as marriage, birth dates of children and occupational history so that individual reminiscence profiles (IRPs) can be constructed. Everybody has lived a life unique to them. Assumptions cannot be made as to experiences and preferences. Not everybody will have liked Gracie Fields, enjoyed riding on a tram, and struggled during the 1930s! We need to be aware of an individual's life-style, habits, interests, likes and dislikes. Their life history can then form the basis of reminiscence activity. It is undeniably true that past events are stored in our mind in relation to personal experience, and so awareness of personal history is necessary to bring the reminiscence experience alive for the individual. There is no point in trying to encourage a 65-year-old who went regularly to the cinema during the 1940s to remember films starring Rudolph Valentino from the 1920s. Although the person may be aware of Valentino from general knowledge gained at a later date, it will not be a genuine reminiscence experienced by that person and uniquely meaningful to them. General knowledge quizzes may be useful in their own right but they are not reminiscence.

The use of IRPs helps us to appreciate the age of those engaged in reminiscence in relation to one another and to the topics being discussed. In a group of 'elderly people' ages may range from 60 to 90. Their recollections of the same event or period will be very different. The 60-year-old, for instance, would have been a child at the start of the Second World War, and may recall being evacuated, whereas the 70-year-olds may have been serving in the armed forces. Only those in their late 80s and 90s are likely to have any recollection of the First World War.

Getting started

Well run reminiscence sessions, whether in groups or with individuals, need enthusiastic, highly-motivated facilitators. In practice this usually means one or more members of staff, although successful sessions have often involved volunteers or relatives.

It is a good idea to designate someone as reminiscence co-ordinator, with the job of collecting old pictures, objects, postcards and records and gathering information on subjects of interest to clients from relatives, libraries and museums. Much useful reminiscence material on topics such as royalty, famous people and transportation is collected together in the *Nostalgia* series by Winslow Press.

When the people participating in the reminiscence session have memory impairments it is important that the group leaders know enough about the topic to provide prompts and cues to aid remembering. It is not enough to show a picture of a film star and hope people will remember who it is. It is essential to have some knowledge of what films the star was in and when.

Milestones or 'Trivia'

When encouraging people to talk about their past it is wise not only to focus on the 'milestones of history' — famous dates and people — but also to concentrate on how life was lived for the majority of people. In fact reminiscence sessions come alive when it is everyday 'trivia' that is being talked about. Not everybody took an interest in current affairs and appreciated mass entertainment. We must also be aware that the media were not as invasive, global or efficient as they are today. Events in far-off places will have held little interest for the majority of ordinary people. Many incidents which, with the benefit of hindsight, are now considered important may not even have been widely reported at the time.

Overall, it is important that professionals working with elderly people are informed historians, drawing not only on information from books on everyday life in past times (of which there are plenty), but also on the local history of the town and region. Information on events and experiences of people in the past serves as a trigger for the unique experiences and reminiscences of each individual which are ultimately more fulfilling than remembering the facts of a particular situation or event.

Reminiscence on a one-to-one basis

One-to-one sessions may be best for those with sight or hearing problems. Care staff and family members can encourage the individual to reminisce about important personal events by using personal memorabilia such as photos (where applicable), favourite ornaments and clothing.

One-to-one reminiscence is important when a person's life circumstances change, for instance if they have to move from their home. Recollection of earlier life experiences and achievements is important in easing the transition from the familiar to the new, and in giving those newly in contact with the person a sense that they are working with someone who has a meaningful past, even if their present abilities are impoverished. As the individual's memory deteriorates it can be reassuring to have other people reinforce the fact that they have lived a valuable and interesting life.

Keeping things going

In day centre and residential settings the concept of active reminiscence can be expanded on considerably by making use of relatives, friends of clients and volunteer helpers, as well as staff. Trips to former places of work, retirement groups and so on can be arranged. People with interests in particular areas may like to visit museums and concerts. There has been great development in the area of local history, and museums often have a local history section from which they are willing to lend items; they also give talks or provide temporary displays in residential settings for those who cannot get out to visit.

There are a number of drama groups and history workshops who will visit establishments and lead reminiscence 'plays'. So often a reminiscence session is little more than photographs of 'flat irons', 'clothes pegs' and a talk about 'what you did during the war'. Reminiscence can be a stimulating experiential event. With a little thought and a lot of enthusiasm reminiscence experiences can be imaginatively created. Rather than simply turning the television on in a lounge, close the curtains, place the chairs in rows and hire a video of a classic 1940s or 1950s movie. In this way a visit to the cinema has been recreated. You can advertise the 'showing' throughout the home or day centre to promote the special nature of the event, and even have an intermission when staff serve cold drinks and ice-cream. The people may still be watching television, but the activity has taken on an entirely different feel.

Alternatively, rather than having the radio or record-player on as background music, why not create the atmosphere of an afternoon tea dance or a 'big band' dance hall? With appropriate music, staff wearing the dress of the period (easily hired from theatrical costumers or 'fancy dress' shops) and drinks served from a bar or by 'waitress' service, elderly confused people can be encouraged to dance and converse with each other as they would have done in the past. When one of the authors saw such an event in a day centre for seriously confused people he could not help but be impressed by how alive the room seemed. The babble of conversation and noise of laughter was a joy to hear, and whilst understanding and the content of speech remained confused this paled into insignificance alongside the happiness, social involvement and spontaneity generated by the experience. This was far removed from a reminiscence session based on questions and answers.

Conclusion

Reminiscence can be an enjoyable age-appropriate activity for many elderly confused people and, as it is a pastime indulged in by 'normal' people, possesses no overtones of stigma nor, in truth, of 'therapy'. Published materials should be used as a starting-point, so as to encourage others to collect locally relevant materials and for the elderly people to contribute their own mementoes, such as photo albums and souvenirs. The elderly people's own reminiscences should direct the activity. The pace of the session should be determined by the ability of the elderly people to express their reminiscences and talk about the materials on display. Never rush through an entire topic when a couple of items or a piece of music may have generated a wealth of enjoyable memories. Creative practice not only benefits the elderly client, but reduces the possibility of staff becoming bored with and reluctant to organise reminiscence activities.

Finally, it is essential that staff know each person as an individual with a unique personal history. The development of IRPs can be encouraged by each client having a life-history book which details their life development. However remember this is a guideline. In some instances such action may conflict with individual need, as certain people may see this as an invasion of privacy. As always, good practice is based on choice, not regulated prescription. Overall, reminiscence is justifiably a popular activity.

REFERENCES

Butler R N, 'The Life Review. An Interpretation of Reminiscence in the Aged', *Psychiatry* 26 pp 65–76, 1963.
Coleman P G, *The Aging Process and the Role of Reminiscence*, John Wiley, Chichester, 1986.

CHAPTER 15

Pam Enderby

Promoting Communication in Patients with Dementia

*T*he ability to communicate is the result of the ability to receive, retain, interpret, formulate, encode and express an idea; therefore cognition, sensory, neurosensory, neurophysiological and neuromotor systems are tested to the full in just this one activity. It is not surprising that patients with dementia frequently have disorders of communication, considering the complexity of that process. These disorders may demonstrate themselves in different ways.

Many speech therapists have been questioning whether they have a role to play in the management of dementia. This chapter will argue that there is a role, but this should be carefully defined. Although specific expertise in this area is desirable, the general skills of a speech therapist can be of great assistance in the management of communication disorders related to dementia. Speech therapists traditionally have the roles of assessing, diagnosing, treating, educating and counselling of those with communication disorders, and certainly, although each aspect is modified in the area of dementia, one can still follow this pattern.

Assessment

There is no single assessment of speech and language which can describe, identify and discriminate the verbal deficits associated with the different

Table 15.1
Communication
strategies and
problems

Communication associated with normal elderly people

- ■Usually have good content of semantic memory (memory for meaning of words)
- ■Good inferencing and association
- ■A reduction in the generation of new ideas
- ■A delay in the access to vocabulary
- ■Grammar is well preserved
- ■Improvement of performance on language tasks, given time

Communication associated with aphasia

- ■Have difficulty with linguistic comprehension, particularly with words which occur less frequently and highly abstract language
- ■Have difficulty with linguistic expression
- ■The grammar and the vocabulary are both vulnerable
- ■There is a willingness to participate in the communication and an attempt to repair errors in communication
- ■Non-linguistic expression and behaviour may be spared

Communication associated with depression

- ■Reduced motivation
- ■Poor concentration
- ■Slow responses
- ■Reduced responses
- ■May relate better to animals
- ■Variability of response
- ■Lack of gesture
- ■Little willingness to communicate

Table 15.1 *continued overleaf*

Table 15.1
(continued)

Communication associated with dementia
■The content of language is affected before the form ■Lack of sensitivity to context ■Breakdown in logical relationships ■Poor associative reasoning (problem solving) ■Random topic initiation ■Grammar may be spared

dementing conditions. It is possible that there will never be one. The speech and language assessment should be seen as part of the overall assessment of the client, contributing information to the general picture which may or may not result in the diagnosis of dementia.

It is important to assess the type as well as the number of errors. Additionally, the way that a patient tries to repair communication difficulties can be indicative of the nature of the underlying problem. This will indicate awareness of communication breakdown, the degree of stress that this causes and the other skills that are available to the person in order to try and remedy the situation.

It is also important to be familiar with the common problems associated with communication breakdowns, so that dementia can be discriminated from other disorders. A brief summary of the main communication strategies used by normal elderly people, compared to three clinical conditions where communication problems are common, are presented in Table 15.1.

All readers will realise that, in fact, patients may frequently have more than one type of problem. Thus an aphasic person may well be depressed, or a demented person may have some degree of additional specific aphasia; however the general guidelines may be of assistance. One will see from this that assessment techniques can only really assist us with eliciting some of these behaviours, which may help us to form a diagnosis with regard to the type of communication breakdown. Those studying the language of patients with dementia see a pattern in its order of symptom presentation. The content and function of speech is often affected before the actual sounds of speech. Word order and grammar often remain relatively intact. A patient may be able to speak more readily when asked direct questions, rather than being able to initiate conversation. The patient will also have more difficulty with defining words, rather than naming objects.

Management of Speech and Language Problems

One of the most vital roles regarding the management of people with dementia is easing the burden on carers by assisting them with techniques which will facilitate better communication with the sufferer. The efficacy of speech therapy techniques with specific disorders associated with language dysfunction of dementia patients is still unclear. It would seem that teaching carers and relatives techniques which they can use in a consistent way has a more direct and long-lasting effect, and it may be that some techniques will help patients who have, in addition to their dementia, some specific language disorder.

Ways of assisting comprehension

The relatives and carers may find it helpful to use the following key points to improve communication. But therapists must be prepared to do more than just list these strategies. Role-playing, group practice and example are required if the message is to be put into practice.

1   Reduce conflicting stimuli. Advise relatives to reduce distractions if it is necessary to discuss anything of importance. For example, turn off the radio and television, or, if the demented person is self-preoccupied (eg. fiddling with something on their lap), take their hands and speak directly facing them.

2   It has been found to be helpful to raise the voice slightly at the beginning, to gain attention. It is also necessary to speak facing the demented person, ensuring that eye contact is kept.

3   Slow down the speech slightly so that it is easier for the demented person to process what is being said. We all tend to speak too rapidly, particularly with those we are more familiar with.

4   Reduce the length of the sentences, trying to use simple grammatical structures; ensure that one bit of information is given at a time.

5 Use different ways of saying the same thing, so that the patient is given the same bit of information in two or three different ways.

6 Reduce possible confusions. Do not use terms like 'he' or 'she', but use the names of the people that you are talking about. Be very specific with regard to places and time and give more prompts with regard to what you are talking about.

7 Do not change the subject quickly; introduce the topic that you are going to talk about carefully before extending the conversation. Use gesture if this will elaborate and not confuse. Point to pictures or things when you talk about them, to help the person to remember.

8 Be realistic; comprehension and confusion will be worse if the patient is emotionally upset or tired. It is not worth trying to introduce important conversations at such times.

9 Avoid open-ended questions, such as "What shall we watch on television?" It may be better to ask "Do you want to watch *this* or *this*?"

10 Using a quiet, slow way of speaking can be soothing and reduce agitation. This can be useful even if the person is not understanding the context of what is being said.

Ways of assisting expression

1 Encourage the person to communicate in whatever way is appropriate.

2 Assist the person to control the conversation by reminding them of what they have said; for example, repeat what they have said immediately after them. You could change the words slightly if necessary.

3 Encourage gesture, such as pointing or thumbs up.

4 Listen to the intonation. This may be communicating more to you than the words themselves. You may gather from the intonation and the pitch of the voice whether the patient is telling you about something happy or sad, even if you cannot understand what the rest of the message is.

5 Encourage the patient to verbalise when they are doing something; for example, encourage them to say "I'm going to have my dinner" just before mealtimes, or "I'm going to walk down the garden" just before that activity. Try to include the demented person in the conversation, because although this is very difficult it may prevent them becoming depressed and withdrawn, which can only make problems worse.

6   People with dementia do very much better with a familiar routine. If it is necessary to change a specific verbal behaviour, then a consistent approach should be taken and this be adhered to by all those caring for the person.

7   Even when the demented person is talking what is apparent nonsense, do take some time to show you are attending and listening.

Care support groups

Many districts have support groups for the relatives of individuals with dementia, and the speech therapist can be very valuable in these groups. It is possible to do role-playing to establish the true nature of some of the ways of improving communication, for example practising speaking slowly, looking at how to simplify language, really understanding what an open question is and how to alter this. These are concrete activities that can be used as a task for the group to work on and can in themselves promote some cohesion within the group.

Conclusion

The value of specific treatment of speech and language disorders in dementia remains a hotly debated issue. However it is essential to remember that speech therapists, with their specialist skills and knowledge, have a role in the assessment, diagnosis and management of people with this disorder. Their training with regard to promoting and facilitating good communication is the very kind that the carers need to have access to.

FURTHER READING

Bayles K and Kaszniak A, *Communication and Cognition in Normal Ageing and Dementia*, Taylor & Francis, Philadelphia, 1987.

Activity and Stimulation Therapies

*I*nvolvement in enjoyable and meaningful activities is often minimal for the dementia sufferer. The previously enthusiastic gardener or avid bridge player may become excluded from activities which take them longer to carry out. Sometimes people exclude themselves from activities if they are aware that they are not as skilful at a task as they used to be.

It is a great shame that, as a person's abilities become restricted, the range of experiences and activities open to them is rapidly eroded. This need not be the case and, indeed, involving dementia sufferers in social and physical activities may enhance their abilities and boost self-esteem. For most of us, being actively involved in work and the routine tasks of everyday life as well as in hobbies and pastimes gives us an important sense of being in control of our lives. Allowing dementia sufferers the opportunity to be involved in life in the same way is essential if they are to be accorded the dignity and respect they deserve as adults.

Unacceptable Activities: What to Avoid

Thankfully, as good care practices are developed and expanded in settings where dementing people are cared for, unimaginative and irrelevant forms of stimulation are on the decline. None the less, at times, the following activities have been noted. Who do you think chose these activities and enjoyed them most — staff or clients?

●*Neighbours* and *Top of the Pops* on television

- Radio One
- Madonna records at a ninetieth birthday party

Although it is acknowledged that staff can be under a great deal of stress at times and may feel the need to 'escape' with half an hour's television (*see more about staff stress in Chapter 24*), activities need to be planned with clients' interests and abilities in mind. Only the most able clients will have sufficient concentration to be able to enjoy programmes on the television left on in the corner of the lounge where many people sit and where a dozen conversations may be going on. Television should be available in a designated lounge or in individual bedrooms for those who particularly enjoy it. Overall, televisions should be used minimally.

If television is to be used, try to make an event of it. Hire videos of interest to the clients, use a large screen such as those used in bars, make sure everyone has their glasses and can see and hear. Have group leaders who can encourage the more impaired people to take note of what is happening. The same applies with records and radio. Imagination and enthusiasm will ensure that they are used to stimulate and interest clients and that the material used is age-appropriate. Just playing the radio or leaving the television on in the corner of a room all day is no substitute for creative activities and in many instances is worse than nothing, because ideas for alternatives are not developed.

Individualised and Age-appropriate Activities

Activity programmes are often planned by staff in day care and residential settings. These are normally group activities such as singsongs, cooking groups, discussion groups, RO and reminiscence activities.

Involvement in a group activity for its own sake will not promote a sense of well-being or self-esteem in an individual. For that, the activity has to be relevant to the interests in their life. It is crucial that a careful assessment is made of each individual's work and domestic interests as well as hobbies and leisure pursuits. Not everyone will have enjoyed bingo or appreciate the music of a particular era. However, it is important that we do not prescribe continued involvement in previous interests and hobbies as to do so may cause distress if previous standards were higher. Reference can be made instead to previous habits and personal characteristics in order to promote meaningful occupation. The opportunity to pursue activities on an individual basis should be encouraged, perhaps with the support of family, friends or volunteers. Of course in settings with few staff it is not always possible for activities to take place on a one-to-one basis. None the less some provision for this should be seen as a priority and, at the very least, programmes should be reviewed and rotated to incorporate everyone's interests on a regular basis.

Table 16.1 highlights the importance of evaluating a person's previous interests and activities in order that meaningful opportunities are made available, to allow them to live a life which is of value to them.

Opportunity and Choice

It is essential that we appreciate that opportunity is only one side of the coin, the other being choice. This of course means that people have the choice of doing nothing. It is not a problem if people wish to sit around, the issue is whether they have opted to be inactive having been given the opportunity to be occupied. Nevertheless being involved and stimulated by something does not mean that the person needs to be physically active. For some, reminiscing alone, sitting by a street window watching passers-by, smelling the products of someone else's baking session or having the cat on their lap can be positive and beneficial experiences. It is important to know whether someone enjoyed passive, sensory experience and what they enjoyed most, so that this can be encouraged and maintained.

Maintaining Life-style Skills

The activities discussed so far can, on the whole, be described as hobbies or pastimes. However life, even in retirement, is not solely geared to being entertained. Many of those in their 70s and 80s worked a six-day week and had few labour-saving devices to aid their domestic chores.

I am not advocating that previous working lives be mimicked in day centres or residential homes, but it is important to remember that self-worth can involve taking pride in caring for a home or for other people and doing a job well. 'Being independent' when living at home, in terms of doing one's own shopping, cooking and cleaning, regardless of the number of hours it all may take, will usually take priority over indulging in a hobby. The same applies to those who are in residential settings. Bathing and dressing oneself is preferable to allowing someone else to do it, even if that means missing a singsong.

Client	Cognitive impairments	Previous life-style and interests	Current activities
Miss D	Mild language comprehension and memory problems	Former music teacher, enjoyed piano, violin and cello concerts, opera	Goes regularly to concerts with her home help, talks to family and friends about music, buys records
Mr H	Moderate memory problems, some dyspraxia, misidentifies familiar objects	Keen gardener, had own allotment for vegetables, fishing	Day centre staff dug small area of ground to grow vegetables; Mr H directs staff on what to grow and how to sow and weed
Mrs J	Severely impaired, unable to make needs known	Cats, usually had two, house plants and flowers, liked perfume and make-up	Loves floral bubble-baths, enjoys nails being painted; staff member brings cat in and Mrs J will stroke it

Table 16.1 Individually planned activities based on previous interests and current cognitive impairment

Thinking about activity and stimulation for clients needs to take account of their priorities in the areas of daily living and self-care, so that they feel they are being given the opportunity to maintain some of the habits of their day-to-day lives. This means that relatives and care staff may have to adjust their own standards. In a residential home, for example, it is more important that Mrs Jayram makes her own bed and dusts her own ornaments if that is what she has always done and wishes to continue. 'Hospital corner' neatness when making a bed is not necessary: if the task really needs to be redone, someone can finish it off discreetly at a later time.

Activities and Risk

Some of the clients we work with may be interested in activities which relatives or carers feel are dangerous or unsafe. If the person shows no interest in smoking because they forget to buy cigarettes, for instance, carers are often relieved and do not promote the activity. But what if the person retains enthusiasm for something that relatives or care staff think is 'unsuitable'?

It has to be remembered that individuals with dementia are adults with the right to make their own choices about how to live their lives, as long as this does not put other people at risk. Sometimes the severity of someone's problems may put them and others at great risk. However, with skill and imagination on the part of carers, this can be minimised and activities can still be enjoyed. It is important that carers are not judgemental and avoid imposing their own ideas of suitable activities on the lives of their dementing clients or patients.

Mr Andrews had, throughout his adult life, enjoyed drinking a whisky and ginger in the evening before retiring to bed. He had become increasingly forgetful over the preceding two years. His wife now noticed that he tended to forget that he had had his evening drink and would ask her to pour him one. The result was that, on some evenings, Mr Andrews would have five or six whiskies and, on others, a major row would ensue between him and his wife. His wife wanted to stop her husband drinking altogether, but eventually found that the best strategy was to give her husband a small whisky and ginger on the first two occasions he asked for it and, if he asked again, to give him ginger on its own. Since Mr Andrews had never been a heavy drinker and it was memory impairment that was leading him to forget that he had already had a drink, this seemed to be an acceptable solution. The effect of the memory problem was dealt with, rather than his wife preventing him from indulging in an enjoyable activity altogether.

Activities for People with Advanced Dementia

Often this particular group of people benefit less from discussions, group activities, games and trips and are often excluded. However, just because a person appears to be non-responsive, this does not mean that such is the case. A wide range of approaches to sensory stimulation are available and, with imagination, may be enjoyed by severely impaired people. All of us have sounds or smells that are evocative and meaningful to us, and appreciate particular tactile experiences. Massage using scented oils may be appreciated by some clients; having one's hand held or being hugged by someone close may be particularly important for a group of people whose experience of touch may be cursory and task-orientated during dressing or bathing.

People who are bed- or chairbound may enjoy sheets, pillows, cushions and clothing of varying textures. Experimenting with ripple beds, lambs' fleece underblankets or scented pot-pourri pillows should be encouraged and, if a person has been known to have a particular preference, this should be noted and accommodated if possible. Preferences for particular types of fabric should be borne in mind when buying clothing for someone: Mrs Polak had always liked a particular satin dressing-gown and still seemed to enjoy stroking and smoothing it, even though she was suffering from advanced Alzheimer's Disease.

Favourite music and food should be established so that staff can draw on as wide a range of tastes as possible. Even if there seems to be no change in the person's behaviour when they are dressed in clothes made in a favourite fabric or colour and have their favourite flowers on their chest of drawers, they should at least have the chance to experience former pleasures. We cannot be sure about the extent to which very impaired people can respond to stimulation, but it is wrong to assume that nothing is taken in. Enthusiastic and imaginative staff will be able to think of ways of giving severely demented people the opportunity to absorb some of the pleasures from their world and this needs to be actively encouraged. People deserve to have the choice of experiencing familiar pleasures of life, regardless of the degree of their impairment.

Conclusion

It is important that people with dementia are encouraged to retain involvement and pleasure in lifelong activities and interests, should they so choose. Activity should be planned with the individual in mind, rather than always expecting people to join groups or to be sociable.

Maintaining involvement in domestic routines and daily tasks can be just as important as keeping up with hobbies and pastimes. The sense of achievement involving an ordinary task can mean as much as the sense of pleasure from a 'treat' or leisure pastime.

Creativity and innovation are the key to adapting activities to suit the individual's ability. Even when people are very impaired it is vital that we challenge the idea that 'nothing can be done with them'. Everyone deserves the chance to continue to benefit from some of life's experiences.

PART 4

Common Management Problems

The Management of Aggression

The chapters in this section describe those behaviours that cause irritating, frustrating, distressing demands and troubled relationships. Strain and upset result from caring for somebody who is 'being restless and over-talkative during the day', 'being disruptive at night', 'being unco-operative and resistive', 'causing trouble with neighbours', 'engaging in rude and embarrassing behaviour', or 'having no regard for the feelings of others'. It is easy to see why such behavioural excesses are poorly tolerated. Physical disabilities are rarely perceived as being as stressful. This is not only the case among family care-givers; professional workers also find caring for disruptive dementia sufferers stressful. While the 'pleasantly confused' are welcomed, it can be difficult to find people with challenging behaviours long-stay or respite placements, for the reason that they are likely to have a negative impact both on the smooth running of establishments and on the resident or patient group.

Aggression

Aggression is frightening and potentially dangerous. Whether it is a physical attack or verbal abuse, to be the victim of such behaviour is always distressing. For the carers of dementia sufferers it is necessary to be aware that violent outbursts are not confined to the young, fit and able. A sizeable minority of dementing elderly people display temper tantrums and aggressive behaviour, causing their supporters serious management problems. Acts of hostility are often unexpected and inexplicable. There may be no straightforward and logical explanation for the behaviour, embedded as it is in a confused and partial understanding of events.

However, while aggression is in part a consequence of organic changes within the brain, we cannot divorce the hostile incident from the circumstances within which it takes place. It is also a disservice to the person and an unhelpful approach to management to describe aggression in terms of personality rather than evidence of undesirable behaviour, specific, for example, to threatening circumstances. Aggressive behaviour rarely occurs without reason. The more carers understand about the motives for the behaviour the more able they will be to prevent dangerous incidents. In fact, as aggression is often a reactive problem in response to situations and the actions of others, the issue is often whether supporters can learn new habits and routines.

Possible Explanations

A useful starting-point is to move away from the idea that aggression is a uniform behaviour to a typology of aggressive acts which assists in both understanding and prevention. A typology provides us with a range of descriptive categories which offers possible explanations as to cause. Seemingly unpredictable outbursts of anger or violence can lose their mystery following an examination of potential triggers.

Defensive behaviour

Aggression may be a defensive reaction to threatening intrusions upon personal space. Assisting an elderly confused person in basic self-care tasks such as dressing or bathing may be resisted because of fear or embarrassment. As memory function progressively fails the non-recognition of carers can seriously aggravate the problem.

Failure of competence

Attempts to help the elderly person with everyday activities may be unwelcome as they are explicit evidence of incompetence. Similarly, during assessment, question and answer sessions designed to test memory may be met by extreme annoyance and an abrupt termination of the interview. It is common for confused elderly people to deny or fail to accept their inadequacy or dependence on others as they hold onto a past which is a record of a life lived successfully.

Disinhibited over-reaction

Frustration is at the root of much aggression. For an elderly confused person an unexpected change in routine, a misplaced article of value or a name that cannot be recalled may result in frustration and an outburst of temper which is poorly controlled.

Reality confrontation

Exposing an elderly disoriented person to the painfulness of a present which is characterised by a loss of persons, places and things can result in anger as they attempt to seek security and pleasure in a reassuring past. The practice of reality orientation should be at all times a sensitive response to confusion based on individual need (*see Chapter 13*).

Alarm

Abrupt and rapid approaches toward a confused person, especially if coming from behind or involving unexpected physical contact, can easily result in a hostile act of self-protection.

Misunderstanding events

Trying to make sense of a world through a mist of confusion can easily result in misunderstanding and inappropriate reactions. For example, a frail, confused man may perceive a community nurse who visits regularly as an uninvited and unwelcome intruder or a dementing woman on a long-stay ward may hold a belief that fellow patients are strangers who are interfering with personal possessions and failing to respect privacy. Such misunderstanding can, understandably, be responsible for aggression.

'Adaptive' paranoia

In dementia an 'adaptive paranoid' phase is common. This is not evidence of psychotic illness, but is a means by which the frightening implications of a deteriorating memory are denied. Making accusations against others to explain why items cannot be found or why an arrangement was forgotten can provide external sources of blame for internally caused errors. As such attempts to hide incompetence are early rather than late features of dementia, the accusations may at first appear plausible.

Manipulation

The elderly confused individual may use aggression as a means to manipulate carers and fellow residents in order to get their own way. Such behaviour is likely to be maintained by the success of 'bullying'.

Attention seeking

As violent behaviour may have disastrous consequences, it is a powerful means of gaining attention.

'Secondary' aggression

Aggression may be the unanticipated reaction to a carer's response to contain or control another disruptive behaviour, such as wandering.

It is easy to see that unthinking care practices can exaggerate the likelihood of violent and abusive behaviour, either by failing to prevent the circumstances which give rise to aggressive outbursts or by reacting unwisely to an episode of aggression.

Understanding the Individual Problem

Although at one level it is important to recognise that we can describe the reasons for aggressive behaviour in general terms (eg. defensive, alarm, 'adaptive' paranoia, attention seeking) it has ultimately to be seen as an example of disruptive behaviour *unique to an individual*.

Nobody is aggressive the whole time. Aggression is not a continuous activity. In order to understand what is responsible for triggering a violent reaction we may well need to look at the situations in which it occurs. This involves not only identifying when and where the aggression takes place, but also noting what the person was doing before the incident and what the response of carers was to the outburst. Carrying out a behavioural analysis will enable carers to provide a framework for understanding the problem behaviour (*see Chapter 8*). The process of investigation therefore progresses from categorisation to an individually centred programme of analysis.

The Aggressive Outbursts — Do's and Don'ts

Although we can do our utmost to prevent the likelihood of aggression occurring, nobody is infallible and so management mistakes can be made. In addition some elderly confused people are notoriously unpredictable. As a result carers require knowledge and skills to manage aggression and thereby reduce the risk of injury to themselves, the aggressor and bystanders.

What not to do

Supporters caring for confused elderly people who have the potential to be either physically violent or abusive should be advised:

1 **Not** to be confrontational.

2 **Not** to take personal offence at the assault or accusation.

3 **Not** to raise their voices.

4 **Not** to attempt to lead away the confused person or initiate any other form of physical contact, as such actions can easily be misunderstood or resented.

5 **Not** to approach the person rapidly.

6 **Not** to approach the person from behind.

7 **Not** to corner the confused person, as this will heighten feelings of threat and alarm.

8 **Not** to crowd them by calling for assistance from several members of staff.

9 **Not** to provoke by 'teasing' or 'ridiculing'.

10 **Not** to use restraints.

11 **Not** to show fear, alarm or anxiety, as this can either encourage people to become more violent or serve to agitate them.

If these guidelines are followed the likelihood of carers triggering a catastrophic reaction is reduced.

Recommended practice

For carers to feel confident in their ability to cope with aggressive patients they need also to know what is expected of them at a time of crisis. The following responses, not all of which will be practicable in every aggressive situation, are essential features of effective management:

1 Stay calm.

2 Respect their personal space (this varies from person to person, but at a time of distress a distance of about five feet is a useful estimate). Keep a safe distance and allow the person to remain in their present position. Overall, give the hostile person plenty of room.

3 Provide reassurance that they will not be harmed.

4 If appropriate (or possible) ask or direct other people to draw back and not to interfere.

5 Encourage them to talk rather than act out their anger.

6 Ask the person what is troubling them. Try to identify the reasons for their aggressive behaviour.

7 Listen to complaints. Be flexible and accepting, not rigid or rejecting.

8 Provide alternatives to the behaviour, or divert their attention.

In residential or hospital settings, if the aggressive person's key worker is available, or if they have a good relationship with another member of staff, it is advisable that they take charge of the situation. The key worker will have most knowledge of the patient, and feelings of fondness will conflict with the urge to be aggressive. (Unfortunately, within the family setting, familiarity is less likely to restrain the aggressive dependant, and may even be the reason why aggression is a feature of home life.)

After a while a sympathetic, unemotional, but also firm reaction will invariably encourage the confused aggressor to calm down and possibly even to appear contrite and apologetic. At this point it is wise not to talk about the aggressive outburst, but rather to engage the person in casual conversation somewhere quiet and private away from the site of the incident. If reasonable action can be taken to resolve the issue which triggered the aggression, then such action is obviously advised. If the incident appears inexplicable, investigating the problem through the ABC analysis of behaviour is recommended (*see Chapter 7*).

The victim who is at serious risk

If the confused person is out of control and risks injuring themselves, or if they are attacking, for example, a defenceless and frail patient, staff need to respond quickly and calmly. No more than two members of staff are needed to approach the person (ideally they should once again be well informed and familiar to the aggressor). It is important to ensure that staff are wearing nothing visible which could be potentially harmful to either party if it were to be grabbed.

Staff need to speak in a gentle, yet matter-of-fact manner. The provision of a commentary will minimise the risk of misunderstandings. They need to explain that they are going to separate the aggressor from their victim. If the confused person continues with their violent act, as a last resort the two members of staff should take hold of each arm. There is no need for any other physical contact. The aggressor can be disengaged from the victim, gently led to an area away from others and comforted. If the aggressor remains agitated or does not wish to talk, staff should back away and give them room. A single member of staff can remain to monitor the patient until they calm down. The other carer can return to comfort the victim.

Conclusion

By following these guidelines on how to understand and communicate with a determined aggressive person, staff can avoid a traumatic confrontation at a time when everybody involved is feeling at their most vulnerable.

FURTHER READING

Stokes G, *Aggression*, Winslow Press, Bicester, 1987.

The Management of Toileting Difficulties

One of the most difficult and distressing problems carers have to face is when a confused person becomes incontinent and starts to urinate in the 'wrong' places. Why is it that incontinence occurs relatively early in some people, when for others it represents the end-point of a slow intellectual decline? There is no simple answer to this question, for incontinence is a complex disability.

What is Causing the Behaviour?

Appropriate toileting is an intricate process requiring a number of skills:

1 Recognising the need to urinate;
2 Being motivated to use the toilet;
3 Postponing, within limits, the act of micturition (the technical term for the process of urinating);
4 Locating the toilet (or acceptable alternative);
5 Possessing the physical mobility to get there on time and being able to adjust clothing appropriately;
6 Maintaining goal-oriented behaviour;
7 Initiating the act of micturition when the toilet is reached.

The chain of behaviour can break down at any point because of disease, handicap, personal deficits, environmental factors or a mixture of all these.

While elderly people may experience a need to void urine (that is, to discharge the contents of the urinary bladder) with greater frequency, it is disturbance of the skills chain which results in toileting difficulties.

Incontinence or Inappropriate Urinating?

When an elderly confused person is found to be 'wet', it is essential to discriminate between incontinence as a condition where the person is unaware of their action and inappropriate urinating, which is characterised by a failure to void appropriately following recognition of the need to urinate.

Definition of incontinence

Urinary incontinence denotes a failure of the mechanisms associated with normal storage and voiding of urine so that *involuntary* passing of urine occurs in inappropriate places.

Possible explanations

Localised physical abnormality

Incontinence may result from local disorders of the urinary tract, and thus it is an advisable starting-point, in all cases of toileting difficulty, to request a medical examination. The manner of clinical presentation can result in a diagnosis of stress incontinence (involuntary loss of urine that occurs on physical exertion), urge incontinence (involuntary loss of urine associated with an uncontrollable desire to void which has not been anticipated) or overflow incontinence (the retention of urine with involuntary overflow). Consideration should also be given to the problem of constipation, which is a common cause of urinary incontinence in the elderly.

Secondary nocturnal enuresis

After many years of complete control a person may experience bed-wetting. This may be attributable to sleep weakening effective bladder control.

Loss of bladder control

Incontinence can arise directly from the loss of learned bladder control due to cortical atrophy affecting the frontal lobe. The outcome can be continuous incontinence. Other medical conditions associated with incontinence, such as normal pressure communicating hydrocephalus, are described by Stokes (1987) and Mandelstam (1980).

Definition of inappropriate urinating

Inappropriate urinating is characterised by an *awareness* of a need to urinate which does not result in the voiding of urine in a suitable receptacle.

Possible explanations

Disorientation

Toileting difficulties can arise following a move to new surroundings. A person who is unfamiliar with their environment may roam around the building searching for the toilet until they are compelled to urinate inappropriately. Even when a person has lived for many years in the same house they can become disorientated as their memory loss worsens.

Environment-induced

Even when a confused person is aware of the location of the toilet, the design and layout of a building may make reaching the toilet difficult. The outcome of the 'race' between bladder and legs may depend on the distance which has to be covered and the confidence the aged person possesses to avoid obstacles which may bar the way. If the elderly person suffers from poor eyesight or is physically frail the barriers can appear insurmountable.

Loss of goal-directed activity

A confused person may get up with the objective of using the toilet, but then forget what they had intended to do, leaving them walking aimlessly with no obvious motive until they urinate wherever they may be standing.

Mobility and dexterity

Toileting problems may be the indirect consequence of physical disability. Despite being able to recognise the need to use the toilet, the confused elderly person may be prevented from doing so because of unsteadiness while walking or standing, or because of slowness in moving. Alternatively, the person may reach the toilet in time but will still have difficulties because of dressing problems or an inability to deal with doors, locks, seats, etc. For example, the effects of arthritis or tremor associated with Parkinson's Disease may seriously interfere with the ability to perform movements of the hands.

Emotionality

The onset of toileting difficulties may be associated with the experience of emotional trauma, such as bereavement, rejection or movement to new surroundings. The psychological basis of the problem may be either anxiety or depressed indifference.

Apathy

Continence is an acquired habit, the motivation for which may diminish among confused elderly people as a result of quite minor factors. For example, the prospect of having to leave a comfortable lounge to visit a stark, poorly lit toilet may serve to discourage appropriate toileting.

Attention seeking

Through urinating inappropriately a person who is receiving less attention than usual or an amount insufficient for their needs can manipulate carers and force them to take more notice and give more of their time. Inappropriate urinating may even be used as a means of revenge on those they wish to provoke or annoy.

Over-dependency

Over-concern by a carer may lead to the needless 'babying' of a confused person. The outcome can be a regression to dependent infantile behaviour characterised by 'incontinence'.

Drug effects

Toileting difficulties may be a sign of drug side-effects. For example, they may be attributable to excessive drowsiness caused by the use of tranquillisers, or an unwanted response of a patient to diuretics. Bed-wetting at night may arise following the prescription of night-time sedation.

As can be seen, incontinence and inappropriate urinating are by no means straightforward problems to either understand or manage. Focal brain damage can also result in toileting difficulties when, for example, agnosia leads to a failure to recognise the toilet and similar objects, such as a wash basin or bath, are used instead, or when frontal lobe damage prevents the logical ordering of behaviour necessary for toileting.

Furthermore, during a behavioural analysis, identification of cause may remain difficult. Unlike the situation with other disruptive behaviours which are almost immediately obvious, disentangling the multiple pathway may be hindered by the hidden nature of the problem. It can be difficult accurately to identify an incident of 'incontinence' at the time of its occurrence if, for example, the person is either discreet, indifferent or unaware of their bodily functions. There is no simple solution to the difficulty. Carers will need to be especially observant during the monitoring period. If the reason for the behaviour remains obscure, it is advisable to test various ideas in succession until the most appropriate explanation for the problem is found.

A Multi-modal Approach to Intervention

Wherever a person lives the multiple pathway to incontinence and inappropriate urinating can often be best confronted through the provision of a range of management techniques which are offered as part of person-centred care. This provides a comprehensive management regime which trawls the potential causes of toileting difficulties and offers guidelines for general care.

On admission to new surroundings

To minimise the likelihood of adjustment anxieties and depression on admission to a residential home or hospital the elderly confused person should be welcomed with sensitivity. You must not underestimate the emotional upset and sense of threat experienced when a person is confronted with a breakdown of relationships, loss of home and possessions and disruption of routines.

To reduce the potential for upset there should be a sympathetic build-up to admission with a phased entry to long-stay care. All staff who will be involved with the new resident should be aware of their needs and personal ways. Good admission procedures can prevent the onset of emotionally-related toileting difficulties which can arise within a short period of admission.

Medical examination

Ensure that the 'incontinent' person is examined by a GP so that reversible medical causes can be treated. Routine health screening should be a feature of late life. This is particularly important where dementia sufferers are concerned, as they are often unable to express their health needs. All drugs being taken should be regularly reviewed.

Mobility and sensory handicaps

If someone's mobility needs to be improved, is the involvement of a physiotherapist or chiropodist required? Would walking aids be of use? Is there a need to correct, or compensate for, visual deficits? If a confused elderly person wears glasses, do not automatically assume that they meet current requirements.

Diet

To prevent constipation the elderly person's diet requires sufficient roughage. Regular consumption of fruit, vegetables, wholemeal bread and high-fibre breakfast cereals is recommended. Is there a need to request the assistance of a dietician in the care of the elderly person?

Fluids

Drinking habits should always be observed as there is a need for an adequate daily fluid intake. Some people may drink excessively, while others drink too little. If necessary, maintain an accurate record of intake and output.

Night-time routines

There is a need for care-givers to ensure that their dependants urinate before going to bed, unless a person's habits suggest an alternative routine. During the night, in residential settings, regularly check whether those who are awake are wishing to use the toilet. The decision to wake people who regularly wet the bed so that they can pass urine appropriately must be considered alongside the possible resulting problems of disorientation, resistance and daytime fatigue.

The provision of care

On occasions requests to be toileted are false alarms, often occurring at busy times on a ward or unit, or when a carer at home is occupied elsewhere. As these are likely to represent manipulative demands for attention, reward appropriate non-demanding behaviour with your time. A constructive approach would be to involve dependants in a programme of stimulation and activity which reflects individual need and brings enjoyment and the opportunity for achievement. The outcome will be a decrease in time-consuming demands and an increase in mutually rewarding carer–dependant contact.

In residential homes sometimes the issue is not excessive demands but a reluctance to ask. When staff do not wear uniforms be aware that a resident may be too embarrassed to request assistance in case they mistakenly seek help from a visitor. Also bear in mind that an elderly man may be reluctant to ask for help with toileting from young female members of staff.

It is important to be aware that a person may recognise the need to urinate but be unable to toilet appropriately and thus legitimately asks for assistance. It is a disservice to the individual either to ignore that person's requests because they are equated with attention seeking, or to introduce unnecessary delay, which leads to avoidable and embarrassing incidents of inappropriate urinating.

If elderly confused people are not allowed to exercise their toileting skills because standards of cleanliness and hygiene take on a disproportionate importance for care-givers, there will be an unnecessary increase in dependency as individuals lose the motivation to care for themselves. Give them as much responsibility for their own care as is realistic. Regardless of whether the person is in their own home or in other accommodation they should not be hurried as they attempt to maintain independence. In the short term this may be seen as a time-consuming activity, but overall the benefits of maintaining independence, even for a few months, outweigh the burden of escalating dependence.

Dressing

A person's dressing ability should be assessed and, if necessary, practice in dressing skills should be provided. It may be advantageous to arrange for clothing adaptations. Velcro fastenings to replace buttons can assist confused elderly people who have toileting difficulties because of dressing problems. Always remember, however, that normal clothing should be worn, for personal appearance plays a large part in determining how others react and this in turn influences self-respect.

Toilets

Through the use of signs, symbols, colour-coding and 'pathfinder' arrows, memory-damaged elderly people can be helped to locate the toilet. The use of night lights in the toilet and approach areas not only helps to reduce disorientation, but it also means that accidents are less likely to happen.

In residential and hospital settings there must be an adequate number of toilets, bearing in mind that there will be several peak periods of usage during each day. Toilet facilities should be readily accessible at all times. They should be near (within approximately 10 to 15 yards), and the approach obstacle-free, well-lit and safe.

All doors, whether they be the exit from, for example, a lounge, or the entrance to the toilet, should be easy to open and wide enough to allow entry using a walking frame. They should not be heavy, as this will present a formidable barrier to progress. Nor should they be spring-loaded, as there is a risk that they will automatically rebound upon slow-moving residents passing through.

With regard to the facilities in the toilet area, the toilet seat should be sufficiently high to make it easy for residents to get up and down. Handrails at either side of the toilet for extra support would be advisable. The toilet area should be private, warm and have plenty of room for manoeuvring walking aids. To protect dignity the toilet should not be sited opposite the door. The presence of a call system by the toilet creates a sense of confidence.

By providing a global response to toileting difficulties the multi-modal approach has shown itself to be a successful management strategy.

Therapeutic management

Therapeutic options are also needed for working with confused elderly people who are urinating inappropriately. An approach worth considering is daytime habit retraining.

Daytime habit retraining

When the elderly person's pattern of micturition guides a toileting programme, this is known as habit retraining. It can be of benefit for those people where inappropriate urinating arises because of severe mobility or memory problems which prevent independent toileting ever being a realistic goal.

The objective is to remind the aged person to void at intervals which will anticipate episodes of urinating in order to produce an acceptable toileting rhythm. By sensitively checking at regular intervals whether a person is wet or dry and recording the information on a Habit Retraining Assessment Chart (Stokes, 1987) a pattern of micturition may be revealed. If a pattern exists, then habit retraining takes place by allowing the person to void before the times inappropriate urinating was consistently identified. In this way the programme of checking and toilet prompts is amended to meet individual need.

Severely confused people who unfortunately do not reveal a pattern of micturition must still be kept dry. As habit retraining cannot be practised it is advised that a rigid toileting regime be implemented at regular intervals throughout the day. Other therapeutic responses to toileting difficulties are discussed in Stokes (1987).

Conclusion

Toileting difficulties are complex disorders, yet, as has been shown, they should not be regarded as the inevitable outcome of dementia. During a period of monitoring and recording, when an understanding of cause is developed, sensitivity is required. Incontinence and inappropriate urinating are intimate behavioural deficits, so that assessment and management can easily generate feelings of embarrassment and threat if care is not directed towards promoting respect and understanding.

REFERENCES

Stokes G, *Incontinence and Inappropriate Urinating*, Winslow Press, Bicester, 1987.

Mandelstam D (ed.), *Incontinence and its Management*, Croom Helm, London, 1980.

Controlling Disruptive & Demanding Behaviours

*I*n this final chapter on common management problems the focus is on those actions which introduce great strain into the care setting, namely wandering, screaming and shouting and repetitive behaviour. Caring for an elderly confused person can be challenging at the best of times as they slowly lose touch with reality and become less able to carry out basic everyday tasks. However the appearance of difficult and anti-social patterns of behaviour can make sympathetic care seem an impossible goal. Once again, what is needed is a thorough understanding of cause in order to promote tolerance and guide effective intervention.

Wandering

Wandering is a common occurrence in dementia and, because of the risk of serious falls, road traffic accidents and exposure to extreme weather, can cause great concern among carers. Fears for the welfare of the person who is wandering can become acute, as a watchful eye cannot always be guaranteed. Moreover it is misguided to assume that most residential homes and hospitals are designed to contain in safety those who frequently wander and get lost. They are not. Staff can therefore be placed under strain and become anxious about their responsibility to protect residents or patients.

This can easily lead to over-concern and to the idea that restriction of activity is the only responsible reaction to instances of *supposed* wandering. The first question to be addressed prior to intervention must be: 'Is this person wandering?'

Definition

Wandering is a determination to keep on the move, either in an aimless or confused fashion, or in pursuit of an indefinable or unobtainable goal which results in an inability to return. From this definition it is clearly not always the case that an elderly confused person who walks around the home or appears unaccompanied in the street is wandering. Nevertheless, because they cannot provide a well-argued reason for their presence, as an alert and competent elderly person would more easily do, these people are often labelled as 'wanderers' and whisked back to where they came from in order that a protective eye can be kept on them.

If a tendency to wander is identified it is of use to clarify whether the elderly person wanders solely within the home without risk to themselves or others, or whether they venture outside in a hazardous fashion. Clearly the former behaviour pattern can be tolerated, given that there is little cause for alarm, although in *all* cases efforts should be taken to identify cause. The absence of risk should not generate complacency and inertia.

Possible explanations

Separation anxiety

Because of their poor memory for recent events, an elderly confused person may wander because they have no recollection of how long a carer has been gone, where they have gone to, or any message to the effect that the caring relative will soon return. Wandering occurs as efforts are made to locate the reassuring presence of the carer.

Searching

An attempt to find something which, or somebody who, is unobtainable. Seeking a deceased loved one, usually a parent or spouse, is common. On occasions, a person may no longer recognise the home in which they live as their own and insist on leaving.

Boredom

Many confused old people lack exercise and interest and so could be wandering out of sheer boredom. If the confused person has been used to a high level of activity the tendency to wander can put carers under extreme pressure.

Loneliness

The isolated dementia sufferer who lives alone may be wandering because of loneliness. However, loneliness cannot be remedied by just anyone's company. Thus wandering may occur even in residential settings where other people may be seen as strangers. The elderly person who has lost a spouse is more likely to manifest this type of wandering.

Physical discomfort

As walking can ease discomfort, a confused person who is in pain due to earache, toothache or constipation, for example, may start to move around a building and be regarded as 'wandering'.

Coping with stress

If a person used to obtain relief from stress by taking a brisk walk or a long stroll, wandering can be a confused continuation of this life-long pattern of coping.

Apparently aimless wandering

A person may get up with a task or plan in mind, but then forget what they had intended to do, leaving them wandering aimlessly with no obvious motive. On occasions a knowledge that there was a reason which can no longer be recalled can result in the person wandering around the home becoming increasingly agitated.

Disorientation

Wandering can start following a move to a new environment. Because of the difficulty in storing new information as a consequence of short-term memory damage, unfamiliar surroundings are likely to remain strange and perplexing. The result is that confused elderly people may roam around the building searching for their bedroom, the toilet and so on. Even when a person has lived for many years in the same house they can become disorientated as their confusion worsens.

Night-time wandering

Confused wandering can be most marked at night. The hours of darkness and silence can easily disorientate the elderly person with memory loss, for they rely on information from the environment to keep in touch with reality. A dementing person, waking at night with no recollection of their whereabouts, may start roaming about the building in an effort to seek information and gain peace of mind.

However it is important to recognise that old people do not require much more than five or six hours' sleep at night and thus nocturnal restlessness may not result from insomnia, but be the unwanted consequence of night-time procedures. If an elderly person goes to bed in the late evening, it is possible that they may awake in the early hours of the morning feeling refreshed and having had sufficient sleep, yet be undeservedly labelled as suffering from insomnia which needs to be 'treated'.

Avoidance

A confused, language-impaired dementia sufferer who is unable to voice complaints may seek to escape from unpleasant environmental 'noise'. Sitting by the meaningless stimulation of a television or having to endure age-inappropriate background music can understandably result in a person avoiding these situations. Similarly, ignoring the needs of an individual can result in 'escape' behaviour. For example, a quiet, private man could be placed in day care or reside in a group living unit as a result of dementia in old age and then attempt to escape from such unsatisfactory environmental arrangements. Unfortunately this may be seen by staff as an instance of confused wandering without meaning.

Attention seeking

Because of the potential risks involved when an elderly confused person walks away from a situation, especially if they go outside, such action may be used to gain the attention of others.

Management

The response of staff to wandering can be summarised under five major management headings:

Changing the physical environment

Building familiarisation. The use of signs, symbols, colour-coding and directional arrows can be effective in making the building more familiar. Signs need to be prominently displayed. Simple messages are advisable. Large pictorial signs or symbols should be used along with the written word, for while reading ability may remain comprehension may be lost.

Appropriate lighting. What is familiar during the day can appear threatening and mysterious at night and result in agitated wandering. A solution is to install night-lights in the bedroom and the areas an elderly person may wish to reach during the night.

Behavioural methods

Manipulation of consequences. When it is safe to do so, somebody who is wandering should be denied fuss and attention while they are roaming about. Instead, when they are doing something which is incompatible with wandering, such as sitting quietly or joining in a constructive behaviour, they should be rewarded with staff time and approval. This not only dissuades a person from wandering in order to gain attention, but improves their quality of life by encouraging them to join in activities.

Occupation and companionship

Activity. The provision of age-appropriate occupation may prevent wandering occurring. (*For guidance on providing meaningful interests, see Chapter 16.*)

Social contact. To remedy feelings of loneliness and isolation when a person lives in their own home and is without family or friends, attendance at a luncheon club or day centre or the use of a 'good neighbour' scheme may be useful options. In some areas an outreach resource which enables home sitters to befriend a confused person may be available.

Professional care-givers, whether in long-stay settings or in a person's own home, should not equate talking to dependants with wasting time, nor feel guilty about doing so. It is one of the most important aspects of providing person-centred care. In many ways it is the responsibility of senior staff to ensure that junior nurses, care assistants and home care staff understand that spending time with a confused person is an essential part of the job.

Exercise. Some people who wander appear to have seemingly limitless energy, and so the scheduling of physical activity may help to satisfy the need for exercise. Walks outside in the fresh air are ideal, so, if there is a garden, staff should make full use of it.

Psychological methods

Reality orientation. At times of disorientated behaviour reality testing can be of great importance. All that is strange needs to be explained in detail (*see Chapter 13*).

Distraction. The aim is to get the confused person to forget their intention to wander and divert them into another activity which will absorb their attention.

Collusion. This is an alternative to distraction. If the person is not disturbing anybody and is not in immediate danger, but is likely to get lost if not closely monitored, any potential crisis can be defused simply by staff accompanying them.

Safety and security

The provision of sensible security precautions helps reduce unnecessary risk and allow carers to be confident that a crisis is less likely to develop through an elderly person unknowingly wandering away and getting lost. This is not to imply that a system of protective custody is being advocated. Furthermore placing any restrictions on an elderly confused person's liberty does *not* resolve the challenging behaviour; it simply reduces risk and thereby brings about peace of mind for carers.

Personal information. Providing information such as name, address and telephone number on a tag in a pocket, or placed in a wallet or purse, or even on a label which can be stitched inside their jacket or overcoat, will aid a speedy return home following 'discovery'. However it is important that the information is carried in a way which does not 'signpost' the elderly person as an individual at risk.

Alarms. These can be useful when someone frequently attempts to leave the building and care-givers' time to observe them is limited. Triggered by a small tag fitted into the clothing of a person who wanders, the alarms can be installed at the main entrance or front door and other high-risk exits to alert care-givers when a confused person leaves the building.

However, there are certain issues and questions which need to be addressed when the use of electronic tagging is being considered (*see Table 19.1*).

Table 19.1
Implications of
electronic tagging

Issue	Question
The alarm must be unobtrusive so as not to distress the elderly person, nor disturb the resident or patient group.	Will there be sufficient staff to monitor a discrete alarm which may only be heard in the exit area or, if connected to a master console, in the office? If not, are mobile receivers which staff may carry available?
The electronic tag needs to be attached to clothing.	Is it not possible that the article of clothing could be removed by the confused person, thereby overcoming the alarm system? A danger is that 'tagging' can breed a false sense of security amongst staff.
A 'triggered' alarm system enables doors to be left 'open'.	Could a situation arise wherein a 'tagged' elderly person could lead out confused residents who may remain outside unobserved and at risk?

Another simple alarm system is to connect the opening of the front door to the door-bell. Whenever the door is opened the bell sounds. Such a device is both unobtrusive and 'normal', and can be easily used within a person's own home. If the system is used in hospital settings where, for example, the door to a ward is in constant use, the introduction of a digital code can prevent the bell ringing. The code is displayed by the door, and if it is punched in prior to the door being opened the bell will not sound. As a confused person will be unable to master the procedures, when the bell sounds staff are appropriately alerted.

All in all, while alarm systems may have their place in the delivery of care, they need to be employed with caution, if for no other reason than that they are not foolproof.

Locks. While the locking of doors is not to be encouraged in hospitals or residential settings, if the confused person lives at home the security of the front door may be an important concern. If a carer is to be free of the need to mount a constant watch and have a sound night's sleep without worrying about whether their partner has slipped out of the house under the cover of darkness, securing the front door may be an essential measure.

As confused elderly people have difficulty in storing fresh information and learning new ways, a new lock on the front door can be a significant barrier to wandering outside. The more complex the lock, the less likely it is that the problem will be solved. Locating a lock in an unfamiliar position, such as at the top or bottom of the front door, will make the opening of the door a complicated task. This is an alternative to a lock which is difficult to operate.

A safety measure often used in hospitals is to employ 'baffle handles' which need to be pulled simultaneously in opposite directions. These difficult-to-operate handles help to prevent the possible dangers of wandering, while providing maximum opportunity for physical activity within a designated area. Similarly, the use of digital locks, which can puzzle the more able confused patient who can overcome the 'baffle' system, can be effective. In this instance access *into* the ward is 'open', but to leave the ward requires input of the digital code. Again, this can be displayed by the door for the benefit of visitors and off-ward professionals.

At all times when considering the use of locks or similar barriers the issue of fire and safety must be to the fore.

Environmental modification. Simple environmental changes can reduce the chances of a person wandering through doors which put the elderly person at risk. Painting a door the same colour as the adjacent walls will reduce its interest value and diminish the likelihood that it will be noticed by an elderly person wandering by.

At night, drawing a curtain over a door is an effective means of disguising an exit. As this is not a constant environmental feature the association between door and curtain is unlikely to be established. Thus a confused person may walk around a building looking for the exit with little chance of success. Similarly, attaching a full-length mirror to interior doors, the use of which is to be discouraged, will make recognition difficult. However this needs to be offset against a possible chance of increased disorientation and the risk of injury if, for example, the mirror is not adequately secured.

All in all, when discussing measures of safety and security it is important that:

1   A sense of confinement is avoided;

2   Dignity and the right to liberty should not be disregarded simply because a person is intellectually deteriorated and is unable to exercise sound judgement; one of the most distressing features of caring for a dementing person is to see them banging on a window or persistently pulling at door handles in order to attract attention;

3   Quality of life issues are not ignored simply because the elderly person is no longer a cause for concern;

4   The search for an explanation for the behaviour continues.

Screaming and Shouting

This difficult to tolerate behaviour involves loud and persistent vocalising which is resistant to requests for silence. The noisy confused person may scream or indulge in repetitive singing, calling or meaningless shouting. However a noisy confused person cannot automatically be regarded as a nuisance to be either ignored or rebuked. There may be a justifiable reason for the behaviour (for example, pain, alarm or panic).

Possible explanations

If the behaviour is evidence of a socially disruptive problem, possible explanations include the following:

Sensory deprivation

Constant screaming and shouting may be an effort to provide self-stimulation when living a life characterised by inactivity, boredom and isolation.

Attention seeking

Noisy behaviour can easily be employed to attract attention, for carers understandably attempt to find out what is wrong or try to persuade the person to be quiet.

Nocturnal disturbance

Confused shouting can be most marked at night and can result either from insecurity as the person awakes in surroundings perceived as threatening and mysterious, or from lying awake during the hours of darkness when silence can be experienced as an unpleasant source of sensory deprivation.

Separation anxiety

A confused person may call out constantly for a loved one, having no recollection of their whereabouts despite being regularly reminded.

Stress

Agitated shouting can be an indication that the confused person is upset. The noisy behaviour may be a fear response, or the repetitive singing of a familiar song may provide feelings of reassurance and comfort.

Overstimulation

An elderly confused person sitting in a hectic and noisy room or who is bombarded with repeated instructions may experience an excess of environmental input and resort to either agitated shouting or loud vocalising which introduces into the environment a noise which they are able to control.

The probability of confused shouting can so easily be enhanced by inadequate living arrangements, poor life quality and insensitive management procedures. Features of daily life in hospitals and residential homes which need to be considered are:

1 Bored residents spending most of the time inactive and understimulated.
2 Residents denied meaningful company, despite living with others and in daily contact with staff who, unfortunately, are likely to be task-orientated.
3 Only giving residents attention, other than when staff are 'doing' something for them, when they become difficult or disruptive.
4 Leaving the television on hour after hour, which is experienced as an intrusive and annoying background noise.
5 Depriving elderly people of cherished possessions, which provide both continuity with the past and reassurance, can give rise to feelings of distressing insecurity.
6 Sticking rigidly to a night-time routine, which means residents being put to bed at the same time night after night, regardless of whether they are tired or what their pre-sleeping habits had been before admission, can result in restless nights.
7 Leaving hearing and eyesight deficits unattended, which can condemn a person to a world of increasing silence and darkness, resulting in self-stimulation as the only way to break the monotony of their daily existence.

An elderly confused person who has been poorly prepared for a period of respite care can be understandably agitated and call out for their loved ones or shout in distress.

It is easy to see how problems can arise unintentionally in residential and hospital settings, but when a confused older person lives at home their circumstances can be equally troublesome. Spending hours at a time with little to do, possibly alone and feeling neglected or abandoned, can serve to trigger disruptive shouting.

A relative, under strain from the burden of caring, may feel compelled to respond to their loved one's noisy behaviour in order to restore peace and quiet and avoid the embarrassment of disturbing the neighbours. This increase in attention can result in the unintentional encouragement of the behaviour the carer wishes would not occur.

To summarise, noisy behaviour can be a major challenge both to families and to professional carers. The invasive nature of the difficult behaviour can so easily introduce intolerable strain into the care system, so that breakdown and requests for a change of placement in the interests of others is a common development.

Repetitive Behaviour

Even such a seemingly straightforward behaviour as repetitive questioning requires a thorough understanding of cause. When investigating stressful problems faced by family carers, unreasonable demands are regularly cited. Constantly asking questions may be seen as 'deliberate' attempts to inconvenience or upset the carer, or as an example of a lack of concern for the supporter as they seek moments of peace and quiet during the day. The bond between the dependent person and care-giver can become strained and, on occasions, break down.

Possible explanations

Short-term memory loss

Profound alterations in a person's ability to retain information can lead to repeated requests for information. Unfortunately, once this is received, storage deficits mean that the information is lost and the person is motivated to ask again.

Management suggestions

> Do not rely solely on verbal responses. Use prosthetic aids, such as daily diaries, memory boards and environmental cues. Predictable daily routines will help to reduce uncertainty.

Attention seeking

Repeated questioning can be a means of gaining a carer's attention as questions are answered over and over again. Even though irritation may mount and the conversation becomes increasingly terse, any attention can be 'good' attention.

Management suggestions

> Provide attention when the person is not demanding. Check whether care practice is task-orientated to the detriment of meaningful relationships. Even though reciprocity may be restricted, partners should be encouraged to foster companionship.

Emotional insecurity

The elderly confused person may use repetitive questioning as a means of 'clinging' to the reassuring presence of a carer.

Management suggestions

> Look behind what is being said to uncover hidden meaning and feeling (*see Chapter 21*). Practise person-centred care. Once again, predictable routines and prosthetic reminders can provide reassurance.

Frontal lobe damage

A sign of frontal lobe damage is perseveration, the so-called 'stuck-needle syndrome' (*see Chapter 6*). Repetitive questioning may represent perseveration of words and phrases.

Management suggestions

> Assess for other frontal lobe signs, for example perseveration of action, impulsive behaviour, mood swings. Assessment may require the involvement of a neuropsychologist (*see Chapter 6*). If it is perseveration, abrupt distraction may 'shift the needle'.

Boredom

Deprived of occupation and appropriate stimulation, an elderly confused person may indulge in repetitive questioning as a means of gaining relief from boredom.

Provide age-appropriate occupation which is enjoyable to the individual (*see Chapter 16*). Try to work alongside the confused person and involve them in daily activities, rather than regarding them simply as the passive recipient of care.

Conclusion

Unlike the inevitable progressive deterioration in self-care skills and competence, behavioural disturbance is not an inevitable feature of dementia. However, if socially disruptive behaviours do arise, they can be very hard for care-givers to tolerate.

It has been the purpose of this section to overcome the pessimism which accompanies the onset of these problem behaviours. Reasons can be identified, even though they are embedded within the dementing process, and, with the establishment of cause, remedial action can be taken, bringing relief to both sufferers and supporters.

FURTHER READING

Stokes G, *Wandering*, Winslow Press, Bicester, 1986.
Stokes G, *Screaming and Shouting*, Winslow Press, Bicester, 1986.

PART 5

Emotions

Depression in Dementia

*U*p to 50 per cent of people with dementia may also suffer from depression (Alexopolous *et al.*, 1988). Sometimes the signs of depression are mistaken for signs of the dementing process and the person is denied the opportunity of appropriate help and treatment. Professionals working with dementia sufferers need to have a clear understanding of how to establish the presence of depression and possible explanations for it in a dementia sufferer. They also require knowledge of the sorts of help likely to be effective.

Establishing Depression Among Dementia Sufferers

Signs of depression which professionals need to be on the look out for in their patients and clients are noted in Table 4.2. Where the dementia sufferer is concerned, it is particularly important to be aware that memory problems and concentration difficulties may be exacerbated by low mood. Because the sufferer may be unable freely to report sadness, helplessness, sleep disturbance and so on because of possible expressive language problems, it is important to question families and other carers on the presence of any symptoms of depression, as well as to identify changes in the person's life-style as compared to their usual patterns. The use of some structured questionnaires has been helpful in establishing depression among elderly people. The development of a short form of the Geriatric Depression Scale (GDS) by Sheik and Yesavage (1986), has shown encouraging results in identifying depression among dementia sufferers. It is important to consider recent life events, and the extent to which these may have triggered emotional distress leading to depression. As will be discussed in the next chapter on counselling, using reflective listening skills to try to understand the mood behind confused talk or behaviour is an important strategy to employ where depression is suspected.

Explanation of Depression in Dementia Sufferers

It is difficult to say exactly what causes depression in anyone. It is likely that the cause is multifactorial. However we can broadly consider depression amongst dementia sufferers within the following categories, bearing in mind that there can be one or more contributing factors for any individual.

Biological factors

One study found that 57 per cent of depressed elderly people developed dementia within three years of the depression being diagnosed (Reding *et al.*, 1985). It may be that, in some cases, depression is actually an early sign of dementia and is linked to the same biological changes as the dementing process. Alexopolous *et al.* (1988) consider that, where depression occurs for the first time in late life, it is more likely to be associated with degenerative brain changes than is depression earlier in life. Research findings by Alexopolous *et al.* suggest that depression in elderly people is associated with damage to part of the brain known as the hippocampus, cerebrovascular accidents (CVAs) in the right cerebral hemisphere and reduced levels of chemicals called bioamines. These can all occur in the brain of someone with dementia. Thus in some cases it may be that what appears as a depressive 'pseudo-dementia' is actually the early stages of a dementing process.

Psychological factors

Various psychological theories have been developed to explain the onset and maintenance of depression which are relevant to understanding the emotional distress of dementia sufferers. They include those discussed below, which are expanded on by Knight (1986).

1   The 'learned helplessness' theory of depression was developed by Seligman (1975). The theory proposes that depression arises as a result of believing that events in your life are beyond control. The losses associated with aging, including loss of physical health, bereavement, loss of role associated with a job and, sometimes, loss of a home, can certainly contribute to the

individual's sense of having no control over their life. For the dementia sufferer the inability to control the effects of a devastatingly remorseless disease which may result ultimately in loss of control over the ability to carry out the most simple of tasks can contribute to the onset and maintenance of depression. Not knowing the nature of the disease and how it may progress can create feelings of helplessness and being out of control, as can relatives and carers who try to take over tasks such as gardening or cooking which the person used to take pride in and is struggling to continue with.

Seligman has developed his theory to take account of the person's perceptions of who or what is responsible for the lack of control. Blaming themselves and seeing a problem as likely to occur frequently is more likely to lead to depression than blaming something or someone else and trying to see the problem as a one-off. For instance, thinking something like "I always forget people's names, I'm so useless and stupid" is more likely to reinforce feelings of helplessness and depression than thinking, "It's the memory problem I have which makes me forget names. It doesn't happen with everyone, only people I don't know well."

Depressed people will tend to view *positive* occurrences as being outside their control and happening once, rather than within their control and constituting enduring aspects of their life. Thus a depressed dementia sufferer might think, "I only got dressed by 9 o'clock today because Fred did most of it", instead of "When I take it slowly and let Fred remind me what to do next, I usually manage to get dressed by 9 o'clock."

2   Loss of mastery over and pleasure in life's activities can be associated with the maintenance of depression. Lewinsohn (1974), found that depressed people were not as involved in positively self-reinforcing activities or pleasurable events as non-depressed people. Again it is highly likely that the person with dementia is going to have a reduced chance of being involved in self-reinforcing activities because carrying out many previously enjoyable tasks or hobbies will expose problems with memory, concentration and co-ordination and will be punitive rather than positively reinforcing.

The advancement of the handicapping effects of dementia may mean that the person no longer wants to attend social events for fear of being embarrassed or of embarrassing other people. Withdrawal from formerly enjoyable social activities further reduces the person's chances of being in receipt of positive reinforcement. It should, of course, be remembered that some pleasurable activities are solitary, yet these also will be impaired as the dementia progresses. Reflecting on previously enjoyable experiences, reading or 'pottering about tidying the house' may all be diminished as the person's memory, concentration span and intellectual ability are eroded.

3   In Chapter 14 life review is mentioned. Successful review by the individual of their life's experiences, finding a meaning for those experiences and coming to terms with problems or unresolved conflicts which occurred in the past are thought to be an important part of adjusting to late life. Emotional problems in elderly people may be due, not to current adjustment problems, but to those which have not been dealt with from the past. The dementia sufferer's deteriorating cognitive capacity may mean that this work is left undone, causing frustration, depression and despair.

Personal history

The preceding discussion on biological and psychological factors has assumed that the depression has occurred for the first time in late life and is linked to the biological or psychological consequences of the dementing process. Indeed 50 per cent of depressed elderly people will have experienced their first episode of depression after the age of 60. However, for those who have experienced an earlier episode of depression, there may have been biological or genetic aspects which acted as a predisposing or trigger factor. Learned helplessness, loss of mastery and pleasure and life review problems may also have contributed to the cause and maintenance of depression for different reasons than those associated with dementia. An individual with a life history of recurring episodes of depression may continue to have such episodes even when they are dementing. The original reason may be forgotten, but some individuals seem to have episodes of chronic depression which have become habitual, maladaptive ways of coping. When these people suffer depression during dementia it is sometimes more strongly associated with this life pattern than with the dementing process.

Helping Depressed Dementia Sufferers

Drug treatment

Where an individual's depression is thought to be due, in part or wholly, to biological reasons anti-depressant medication may help. Dementia sufferers do respond to such medication and the most appropriate sorts, which have the fewest side-effects, are discussed in Chapter 22.

ECT

Electroconvulsive therapy (ECT) may be helpful with some severely depressed elderly people, particularly where there is pathological guilt, impairment of activities and interests and agitation (Fraser, 1986). However, because of the possible side-effects of memory loss and confusion, it tends not to be the first treatment of choice for depressed people with dementia.

Psychological interventions

Psychological approaches which have been developed for use with older adults in therapy (Thompson *et al*, 1986), can be useful with dementia sufferers and their carers. The following strategies may help combat feelings of 'learned helplessness':

1   Encourage the dementia sufferer and their carers to view positive experiences and events, such as remembering something or successfully carrying out a task, as being due to the *individual*'s skill and something which *can happen again*.

2   Encourage sufferers and carers to view negative experiences and events as being *beyond the person's control* and *not always likely* to recur.

3   Make positive, realistic statements about the person's skills, interests and abilities in order to promote a sense of self-esteem. Comments like "That colour of dress really suits you," and "Your children are a credit to you; you must be proud of them," may not be remembered for long, but they do serve to counteract thoughts such as "I'm stupid" and "I can never do anything right."

4   It is important to try to counteract problems associated with loss of mastery over, and pleasure in, previously enjoyed routines or activities, whether these were social or solitary.

5   Identify with the individual and their family the sorts of things they used to get a sense of achievement or pleasure from doing.

6   If at all possible, try to reintroduce the previously enjoyable task, activity or experience, with support as necessary.

7   Remember that trying to reintroduce some activities will be disheartening. A former skilled chess player may not wish to re-experience the loss of skills in this area, but may enjoy teaching their grandchildren how to play other more simple board games.

8   Encourage the person to identify a number of achievable daily tasks and activities. *Achievement* of a task while the person is still depressed is more important than *enjoyment* which will return only when the activities have become positively reinforcing and are seen as worth the effort.

9   Encourage the individual, with the help of their carer, to keep a diary of daily tasks and activities and to tick them once they have been done.

Further suggestions on activity and stimulation can be found in Chapter 16.

Counselling skills which involve reflective listening, such as resolution therapy, an approach developed by Goudie and Stokes (1989) which adapts counselling principles for work with dementia sufferers, may be helpful in allowing depressed dementia sufferers to ventilate their feelings, although people with severe cognitive impairments will be unlikely to have the abstract reasoning ability required for life review and coming to terms with conflicts earlier in life. Validation Therapy (VT), a method recently developed by Feil (1982) for meeting the emotional needs of confused people, is based on the individual expressing and re-experiencing past emotions. Such techniques may be the means by which professionals can empathise with and begin to understand the feelings of impaired individuals before putting some of the other psychological strategies mentioned above into action. Resolution therapy and VT are discussed further in the next chapter.

Conclusion

Because of the biological and psychological factors associated with it, dementia may lead to a high likelihood of depression in the sufferer. Awareness of possible contributing factors and knowledge of treatment and intervention is of vital importance. Fundamentally those who work with dementia sufferers and their families must accept that the dementing person, whatever their degree of impairment, has a right to experience and express feelings and to have these acknowledged by the people who work with and care for them. Only by acknowledging this right to experience and express emotions will it be possible to develop our strategies for helping those with feelings which have become distressing and overwhelming.

REFERENCES

Alexopolous G S, Meyers B S, Young R C, Abrams R C and Shamolan, C A, 'Brain Changes in Geriatric Depression', *International Journal of Geriatric Psychiatry* 3, pp 157–61, 1988.

Feil N, *Validation – the Feil Method*, Edward Feil Productions, Cleveland, 1982.

Fraser M, 'Physical Methods of Treatment for Depression in the Elderly', E Murphy (ed.), *Affective Disorders in the Elderly*, Churchill Livingstone, Edinburgh, 1986.

Goudie F and Stokes G, 'Dealing with Confusion', *Nursing Times*, p 38, 20 September 1989.

Knight B, *Psychotherapy with Older Adults*, Sage, California, 1986.

Lewinsohn P M, 'A Behavioural Approach to Depression', R Friedman and M Katz (eds), *The Psychology of Depression*, John Wiley, New York, 1974.

Reding M, Haycox J and Blass J, 'Depression in Patients Referred to a Dementia Clinic: a three-year prospective study', *Archives of Neurology* 42, pp 894–6, 1985.

Seligman M E P, *Helplessness*, Freeman, San Francisco, 1975.

Sheik J I and Yesavage J A, 'Geriatric Depression Scale (GDS): Recent Evidence and Development of a Shorter Version', *Clinical Gerontologist* 5(1/2) pp 165–172, 1986.

Thompson L W, Davies R, Gallagher D, and Krantz S E, 'Cognitive Therapy with Older Adults', *Clinical Gerontologist* 5, pp 245–79, 1986.

Counselling Confused Elderly People

*R*ecently interest has been shown in the emotional world of the dementia sufferer (Feil, 1982; Goudie and Stokes, 1989). When communicating with a confused person it is not always necessary to correct their factual errors as they try to function within the 'here and now'. Instead, attention can be directed toward the subjective world of meaning and feeling which is masked and distorted by the person's deteriorated capacity for intellect and language.

Reality Orientation (RO)

RO is traditionally accepted as a therapeutic method which increases motivation and reduces dependency through the use of cued recall. As Una Holden has already described (*see Chapter 13*) this does not mean that RO is simply a mechanistic technique to improve retention of information. In a model of good practice RO involves social therapies, environmental change, reminiscence and recognition of individual need. It also recognises that poorly expressed emotions and concealed meanings are often present, and these also need to be understood and responded to sensitively.

However RO remains primarily an effective memory therapy. It uses the repeated presentation of verbal information and environmental aids, such as calendars, memory boards and directional signs, to correct confused behaviour and to enhance the elderly person's ability to live as independently as possible within their environment. It is not a therapy aimed at uncovering, understanding and reflecting the feelings which lie behind the dementia sufferer's disorientated speech and behaviour.

Validation Therapy (VT)

Validation therapy has recently been introduced as a therapeutic practice for work with 'old old' confused people (Feil, 1982; van Amelsvoort Jones, 1985), that is, people aged over 80. Practitioners believe that the use of VT represents an alternative to RO in that carers do not seek to correct disorientation and confused speech. VT assumes there is meaning underlying confused behaviour and seeks to enter meaningful dialogue with the person on their terms. The carer is said to be validating the person as they attempt to understand the feelings which are concealed by the confused speech and behaviour.

A major premise of VT, which is based on the concept of life review mentioned in Chapter 14, is that some elderly people are unable to accept the fact that they have not achieved their life goals and have not resolved life's conflicts. Such despairing individuals often become isolated, withdrawn and disorientated. Withdrawing from a present reality in which they have no meaningful role and no future is a means of coping with such emotional despair. Fantasy may be used by disorientated old old people to restore feelings of usefulness and dignity. As the person acts out their imaginary existence and expresses 'unresolved inner conflicts through their disorientation, they are often labelled' as demented and their behaviour is dismissed as being confused and devoid of meaning (Babins, 1988).

In VT confused individuals are given the opportunity to resolve unfinished conflicts through encouragement to 'express' and re-experience their feelings. These feelings are not interpreted or analysed, but accepted and acknowledged as a unique product of their life experiences.

Unresolved personal conflicts are discussed within a group of five or six people. The group is led by a facilitator who raises topics for discussion which usually cover areas such as 'death, family relations, loneliness and disappointments' (Babins, 1988). Topic selection is based on the conflicts to be resolved by the group members. The asking of significant questions offers them an opportunity to describe relevant life experiences.

While VT is an alternative approach to helping disorientated people, it is not appropriate for people suffering from Alzheimer's Disease or multi-infarct dementia, with the possible exception of when the dementia is in the earliest and therefore mildest stages. As Babins has recently written, 'Validation Therapy is intended for those persons who have never been diagnosed as having any type of psychiatric disorders ... This approach would not be used for individuals who have been diagnosed as having primary dementia or an identifiable medical illness known to cause disorientation'. Feil talked of the approach as being appropriate for 'confused' individuals, without explaining that this does not include confusion caused by a dementing illness. Others have erroneously used VT with dementia sufferers.

In the early stages of a primary dementia, sufferers may be aware of their memory impairments and diminishing skills, and choose to retreat from a painful reality, but in time the intellectual and analytical powers necessary for abstract reasoning, insight, fantasy development and the use of defence mechanisms when faced with distressing emotions will become markedly deteriorated and this will mitigate against such voluntary actions.

VT may be of use when counselling seriously depressed, alienated and despairing elderly people who are struggling with various losses and conflicts and have surrendered their hold on reality. In other words, VT may be a valuable strategy to adopt when working with people who are displaying a 'pseudo-dementia' of emotional origin. By allowing them to express their feelings it can give such people 'a sense that they are understood, accepted and respected'. This can result in feelings of demoralisation and hopelessness being at least partially remedied.

However VT remains a relatively untried and unproven method of counselling in terms of both its underlying premises and principles of practice.

Resolution Therapy

Resolution therapy has been introduced recently by Goudie and Stokes (1989) as a companion therapy to reality orientation. Unlike VT, resolution therapy is a method of counselling people suffering from an organic dementia. The underlying premise is that the disoriented messages received and the confused behaviour observed are likely to reflect attempts to make sense of the 'here and now' or represent forlorn efforts to express need (*see Table 21.1*). These

Case	Setting	Confused message/ behaviour	Concealed meaning	Underlying feelings
1	Elderly confused man, in company of son, being escorted out of his flat by two members of staff from the residential home he is entering for a trial stay.	"Where am I going? I am not going anywhere without my cat." (His cat died several years ago.)	I need security. I need the reassurance of my past when life was safe and predictable. I need to be soothed and comforted.	Fear Foreboding Dread Anxiety
2	Confused woman in the corridor of an old people's home, shouting at a 'busy' member of staff.	"This is not my home. I am fed up with this place. Take me home." (Minutes later she urinates inappropriately in the corridor.)	I am looking for the toilet. It is not where I expect it to be. Where is the toilet?	Agitation Frustration Anger
3	Confused man sitting in a day-room. Other patients sitting in armchairs. Room is of a 'waiting-room' design. TV is on.	He starts to move furniture around the room, resisting staff efforts to get him to sit down.	I am bored. I need to be active. I need to feel useful.	Boredom Irritation Discontent

Table 21.1 Examples of confused speech and behaviour which conceal genuine need

Case	Setting	Confused message/ behaviour	Concealed meaning	Underlying feelings
4	Confused chair-bound elderly woman sitting in the day-room of a long-stay psychogeriatric ward.	Calling out the name of her recently deceased husband whose funeral she attended in the company of a nurse.	I am alone. I am insecure. I need to grieve.	Sadness Fear Frustration Anger

Table 21.1   (continued)

concealed meanings are likely to be 'attached' to emotions which, if ignored, can result in behaviour easily labelled as difficult or disruptive. It is not felt that disorientation represents efforts to remedy past troubles.

By using the counselling skills of reflective listening, exploration, warmth and acceptance in the tradition of Rogerian humanistic psychology (Rogers, 1951), professional carers can empathise with the hidden meaning and feelings which lie behind confused verbal and behavioural expressions (level 2 analysis; *see Figure 21.1*). While it has to be accepted that, as dementia progresses, opportunities for counselling or work on acknowledging feelings diminish, overall there is a need for a therapeutic approach which enables us to reach behind a person's memory and intellectual deficits to acknowledge their emotional experiences as they struggle to negotiate and make sense of reality through a mist of confusion.

It is not simply the case that the received message possesses an alternative meaning which needs to be addressed. Of equal importance is that, by focussing on the dementing person's factual errors, we may also be failing to understand or be denying the existence of a related world of feeling and emotion. It is wrong to assume that, just because a person is experiencing a profound and widespread destruction of their memory and intellectual abilities, feeling is also eroded. Emotions are censored and controlled by our intellect, they are not part of our higher cognitive functions. Thus an inability to reason and communicate

Figure 21.1
A model of meaning
and feeling in
dementia

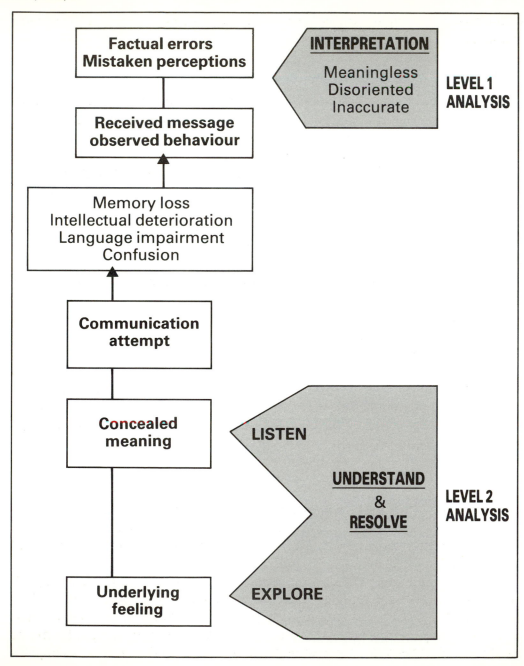

effectively is not an indication that emotions no longer exist or have little significance.

Practice

Resolution therapy is a one-to-one therapeutic approach, to be conducted with sensitivity, patience and tolerance in everyday social interaction. The emphasis is on seeking to understand the concealed meaning and acknowledge the feelings currently experienced. The starting-point is *what*. What is the feeling the person is trying to express through their apparently confused speech or behaviour? By reflecting on the possible feelings behind the confused message (as indicated in Table 21.2) the 'therapist' attempts to understand the world from the point of view of the confused person. Their views are not disputed, nor are they confronted with reality. The 'therapist' attempts to 'flow' with their feelings.

It is essential for staff to understand that they are not analysing *why* the person might be feeling as they do. Rather they are attempting to understand and acknowledge possible feelings. In this way even quite impaired individuals may feel enough at ease to share more about their emotions and the reasons for their feelings will perhaps emerge as part of the 'unravelling process'.

There must be no hint of 'demanding an explanation'. Such action is likely to result in heightened irritability on receipt of a confused response. If the patient process of acknowledging feelings is not going to be employed, then, when the carer is faced with challenging behaviour, techniques such as RO or distraction should be employed.

Resolution

Resolution therapy is ultimately concerned with finding ways to help the person meet their needs and cope with their feelings. These may include verbal and non-verbal acknowledgements as well as modifications to the environment and carer–dependant relationships (*see Table 21.2*).

In counselling, all attempts to reflect and acknowledge feelings experienced by other people must be tentative until confirmation is received. This is just as important with confused elderly people, and so the examples in Table 21.2 serve only as illustrations of the sorts of responses that might be made. Flexibility of reflective response and monitoring reaction to the therapist's

Case continued	Underlying feelings	Reflective response	Resolution
1	Fear Foreboding Dread Anxiety	Maybe you are feeling a bit nervous about coming to Windsor Lodge? Most people do when they visit for the first time.	Reflective responses must be evaluated and modified over time to gain an indication of the type of responses that will lead to the resolution appropriate for each individual.
2	Agitation Frustration Anger	It can be difficult finding your way round Hawthorne House at times. All the corridors look the same. Are you looking for something?	For instance, in example 1 the client may feel acknowledged and just agree 'yes, that's right', whereas in example 3 an appropriate level of resolution could involve collecting the cups in the lounge.
3	Boredom Irritation Discontent	It gets boring just sitting around sometimes doesn't it? Is there anything you'd like to do?	Once an attempt is made to understand the person's feelings, practical attempts, such as modifying their environment or providing a choice of activities, will enhance acknowledgement and help the patient to work through or resolve the expression of their feelings.
4	Sadness Fear Frustration Anger	Are you missing Arthur? Would you like to talk about him?	

Table 21.2 Reflecting feelings — towards resolution

acknowledgements are corner-stones of resolution therapy. The therapeutic challenge is that the process of exploring meanings and feelings, together with attempts at resolution, must continue until the person, by their behaviour and responses, appears more at ease in their world. Of course, because of fundamental retention deficits, this sense of well-being will be, to a greater or lesser extent, temporary. As a result, resolution therapy needs to be a characteristic of social interaction throughout the day whenever indicated, and is clearly not to be regarded as a structured therapeutic activity to be conducted at certain times within a formal setting. Inevitably this develops the enormous therapeutic potential of professional care staff, for only those workers in daily contact and communication with dementing patients are in a position to uncover hidden messages, understand meaning and resolve feelings as the confusion of daily life unfolds.

Conclusion

It is unrealistic to expect family members, especially aged partners, to be able to practise either resolution or validation therapy, for they demand a level of skill beyond that available to the uninformed. It is true to say that, for some relatives, to be asked to re-inhabit the past through their loved one's confusion can be upsetting, as they hold onto a wish to care, and be cared for, in the 'here and now'. However, as Una Holden writes in Chapter 13, it is always common sense to appreciate and attempt to understand the meanings that lie behind disorientated talk and behaviour. It is at this level that family supporters can help both themselves and their dependent relative. To know that responding solely to the dementing person's factual errors and mistaken beliefs (level 1 analysis; *see Figure 21.1*) does nothing to address their emotional needs may be a stepping-stone towards the continuation of sensitive care within the family home.

REFERENCES

van Amelsvoort Jones G, 'Validation therapy; a companion to reality orientation', *The Canadian Nurse* 3, pp 20–3, 1985.

Babins L, 'Conceptual analysis of validation therapy', *International Journal of Aging and Human Development*, vol. 26 (3), pp 161–8, 1988.

Feil N, *Validation — the Feil Method*, Edward Feil Productions, Cleveland, 1982.

Goudie F and Stokes G, 'Dealing with Confusion', *Nursing Times*, p 38, 20 September 1989.

Rogers C, *Client-Centred Therapy*, Houghton Mifflin, Boston, 1951.

FURTHER READING

Feil N, 'Resolution: the Final Task', *Journal of Humanistic Psychology*, 85 (2), pp 91–105, 1985.

Medication in the Management of Dementia

The Medical Approach to Dementia

The diagnostic approach is perhaps most characteristic of medicine as a discipline. A diagnosis is essentially an hypothesis about what is wrong with the patient. It is based on the concept that, by listening to the history, examining the patient and performing necessary investigations, diseases can be identified and named. These diseases are generally due to disturbances of the underlying structure or biochemistry of the body. These in turn may be due to genetic or environmental factors or infection, or a mixture of different causes. Understanding the causes of disease enables rational treatment to be planned. In psychiatry, causes are often multiple and the approach to treatment therefore has to take into account many factors.

The Diagnosis of Dementia

After death, examination of a brain damaged by Alzheimer's Disease shows some shrinkage and microscopic lesions known as senile plaques and neurofibrillary tangles, often in great abundance. The brain's chemical messengers, known as neurotransmitters, are also depleted, especially acetylcholine. This discovery has led to hopes that some kind of replacement therapy analagous to the use of L-dopa to replace dopamine in Parkinson's Disease might be of use. None of the attempts so far have been sufficiently successful to justify widespread clinical use, but agents currently under test (eg. tetrahydroaminoacridine (THA) may partly alleviate some of the symptoms of dementia, although they are unlikely to arrest the progress of the underlying disease.

Multi-infarct dementia is related to stroke illness and high blood pressure. Smoking, unhealthy diet, being overweight and all the factors which increase the risk of stroke also increase the risk of multi-infarct dementia. Attention to prevention, not only through 'life-style' measures but also through the early treatment of high blood pressure, is very worthwhile. Aspirin in very low doses (75 mg per day) may also help in prevention by reducing the liability of the blood to form clots.

Principles of Prescribing

Like any other management, prescription should only follow a careful assessment. It is essential to distinguish between the specific use of a drug to treat a disease (eg. antibiotics in pneumonia or antidepressants in severe depressive illness) and symptomatic use (eg. to induce sleep or reduce 'aggressive' behaviour). In specific use, there are often no worthwhile alternatives to medical prescription, though other measures (eg. physiotherapy for pneumonia, cognitive therapy in depressive illness) may often be used to complement medication. In symptomatic use, however, the alternatives may often be preferable to medication.

Once prescription has been decided on as part of a more general treatment plan another principle — that of minimal medication — is vital. Because medication often has unwanted as well as beneficial effects, it is essential that the minimum number of drugs are prescribed in the lowest effective dose for the shortest time necessary to produce the desired effects. The system of issuing repeat prescriptions for sleeping tablets etc is a great enemy of old people, who may suffer unwanted effects as a result of medication that is too prolonged.

Psychotropic Medication

Drugs which primarily affect the mind are known as psychotropic (literally mind-changing). Some (eg. opium) have been known and used for thousands of years, but the modern range of psychotropic drugs has only been developed over the last 50 years. Psychotropics can be divided into three main groups, according to their main mode of action: antidepressants, neuroleptics and anxiolytics.

Antidepressants

Antidepressants mostly act by restoring depleted levels of neurotransmitters. Many antidepressants share a common biochemical structure of three rings and are referred to as 'tricyclics'. These include amitriptyline, imipramine, dothiepin, doxepin and lofepramine. Their unwanted effects include drowsiness and sometimes a fall in blood pressure on standing up (postural hypotension) which can precipitate falls. Other unwanted tricyclic effects include dry mouth, confusion, constipation and occasionally the precipitation of eye disease (glaucoma) and retention of urine. Taken in overdose they can cause the heart to malfunction. Newer tricyclics like lofepramine and other non-tricyclic antidepressants like mianserin and fluvoxamine have less of these side-effects, though they have their own problems. Less often used are the monoamine oxidase inhibitors. Unfortunately complicated dietary restrictions must be observed if they are to be taken safely, so they have little place in the treatment of the dementia sufferer.

Neuroleptics

Neuroleptics, also called 'major tranquillisers', act mainly on the dopamine neurotransmitter systems in the brain. Their specific use is in schizophrenia. They include drugs like chlorpromazine, haloperidol, thioridazine, promazine, trifluoperazine and sulpiride. They also have a non-specific use as sedatives and tranquillisers and it is for this that they are often used in restless patients with dementia. Because dopamine systems are also concerned in Parkinson's Disease, one of the common unwanted effects of neuroleptics is the induction of a Parkinsonian state characterised by stiffness, trembling, slowness of movement and, sometimes, paradoxically, restlessness. Some drugs, like haloperidol and trifluoperazine, produce particularly strong Parkinsonian side-effects and so dosage has to be controlled very carefully. Others, such as chlorpromazine and thioridazine, are less likely to cause Parkinsonian effects but may increase confusion. Chlorpromazine in particular may also cause postural hypotension. Droperidol is related to haloperidol and has a very marked sedative effect.

Anxiolytics

Anxiolytics, also known as 'minor tranquillisers' and used as sleeping tablets, are the most commonly prescribed of psychotropic drugs. Most of them belong to a group known as benzodiazepines and include diazepam, nitrazepam, flurazepam, temazepam, lorazepam and lormetazepam. Many old people use them to get to sleep, but they also have unwanted effects. They may accumulate and cause over-sedation or 'hangover' effects and patients may become dependent on them. They may also impair memory and performance of complex motor tasks. They may be responsible for falls. There are now strong moves to restrict their prescribing to short-term use as the burden of disability caused by them is recognised.

Drug metabolism and interactions

In old age there are changes in the way in which the body processes (metabolises) drugs which cannot be described in detail here. The effect of most of these changes is to render old people more susceptible to the unwanted effects of drugs and this, combined with multiple diseases and multiple prescriptions, puts old people at special risk of adverse drug effects. For a fuller description of metabolism and interactions, see Wattis and Church (1986) Chapter 10.

Specific Problems

Sleeplessness and night-time restlessness

It is important to exclude specific causes of sleeplessness, for example pain, heart failure and depression. If these are present they should be treated. Cat-naps during the day should be avoided. Adequate exercise and mental stimulation should be provided during the day and stimulant drinks, including coffee and tea, kept to a minimum in the evening. A small warm milky drink and a clear bed-time routine may help. There should not be an unrealistically early bed-time or unrealistic expectations of how long the old person with dementia will sleep. Emotional and practical support to the carer while the dementia sufferer attends day care may also reduce the perceived emotional burden of disturbed nights. When all these measures have been tried, there will remain a minority of demented old people whose night-time restlessness is intolerable to the care-giver. In these circumstances low doses of the more sedative major tranquillisers, such as 10–25 mg thioridazine in the late evening, may be useful. Sometimes this will not be enough and a minor tranquilliser, such as $\frac{1}{2}$–1 mg lormetazepam at bed-time can be added, usually for a maximum of a week.

Daytime restlessness and wandering

If there is a marked increase in daytime wandering or restlessness, causes must again be sought. Is the wandering secondary to depressed mood and consequent agitation? If there is depressed mood, this can be treated with an appropriate sedative antidepressant, such as dothiepin or mianserin. Often this can be given as a single night-time dose, when it has the bonus action of improving sleep. Once again, when all commonsense remedies have failed, the non-specific use of medication may be considered. Very low doses of haloperidol, eg. $\frac{1}{2}$–1 mg twice daily, or higher doses of thioridazine, eg. 10–25 mg up to three times a day, may help. Minor tranquillisers are not much use.

Incontinence

This is rare until dementia is very advanced. In the earlier stages of dementia, toileting difficulties are frequently due to such problems as failure to find the toilet or to medical problems such as constipation or urinary tract infection, which must be tackled in their own right. Most drugs which are alleged to promote continence are likely to increase confusion and rarely contribute much to improving the incontinence. They are best avoided.

Aggression and violence

Violence is rarely unpredictable. Martin Luther King once said (in quite a different context) that violence is the voice of the unheard. This aphorism also applies to the dementia sufferer. An old lady who believes she has to go home to make her (dead) husband's tea or attend to the baby is unlikely to take kindly to the staff member who blocks her way and tells her not to be so silly! This kind of behaviour is fortunately now much rarer amongst professionals of all disciplines, who are trained to try to understand the world from the demented patient's point of view and use a pleasant approach and techniques such as distraction and diversion rather than authoritarian confrontation. With the best care in the world some old people with dementia will become violent. Again it is important to consider whether there may be a medical cause — such as an infection or heart failure leading to a sudden increase in confusion (acute confusional state).

Medication may be needed in an emergency to contain the situation while other measures are taken. Low doses of droperidol by mouth or, in extreme circumstances, intramuscular haloperidol may be justified. Such measures should always be regarded as short-term until better approaches can be devised. In short-staffed long-stay facilities, there may be a temptation to use sedative medication to make life more manageable for the staff. This is a difficult ethical problem for the doctor who often feels powerless to influence nurse staffing levels but does not believe in using sedation to compensate for lack of staff time. The only real solution is the provision of adequate numbers of well trained staff.

Conclusion

The medical management of dementia demands an accurate diagnosis. At present there are no useful specific treatments for Alzheimer's Disease, but measures to prevent multi-infarct dementia have been suggested. When it comes to symptomatic treatment of problem behaviours, it is essential to try to determine and deal with underlying causes. Sedative medication is only one of a range of alternative approaches and, because of the possibility of unwanted effects, should be reserved till other measures have been tried and found to be ineffective.

REFERENCES

Wattis J and Church M, *Practical Psychiatry of Old Age,* Croom Helm, Beckenham, 1986.

Supporting the Families of Dementia Sufferers

*T*he management and care of most dementia sufferers takes place in the community, as approximately four out of five people with dementia are cared for outside hospital or residential settings. Although some of these individuals live alone (mainly those in their late 80s and 90s) the majority live with a member of their family, usually their spouse but sometimes their son or daughter.

Since the average time from the onset of Alzheimer's Disease until death is between five and seven years, and about four of these are spent at home, a considerable burden of caring is shouldered by family members.

The Stress of Caring

What kind of burdens are carers under? How do they manage to look after people who suffer from an illness which may mean at best that a former vivacious and stimulating conversationalist is only able to respond to questions in monosyllables and which at worst requires total care of all their bodily functions? Do carers themselves become ill or do they find ways of coping?

Caring for dementia sufferers can place physical and emotional strain on families and supporters. Often just knowing what the illness is can make caring easier. Sometimes families feel that a dementia sufferer is just trying to get their attention and support and it is not until the condition has been diagnosed that they are able to stop blaming or accusing their relative of deliberately making mistakes. However, all too often, the unremitting burden of care continues after assessment and diagnosis, as one family member is left to care because others live too far away, work long hours or have other domestic commitments.

A substantial amount of work has been done on exploring the sort of strain relatives are under when they care for someone with dementia (Gilhooly, 1984; Gilleard, 1984; Morris *et al.*, 1988).

Problems experienced by carers

The most frequent problems reported by those caring for dementia sufferers include:
- Inability of the dependant to be left alone;
- Disruption of the carer's personal life;
- Inability of the sufferer to hold a sociable conversation;
- Lack of self-help skills such as dressing, feeding and bathing;
- Loss of sexual intimacy and emotional support from the dependent partner;
- Continual questioning;
- Incontinence;
- Demands for attention.

The relationship between sufferers and carers

The nature of the previous relationship seems crucial when considering how carers cope with dementia in a loved one. Where the relationship between husband and wife has not been close, the strain of caring can be greater. On the other hand, if the relationship has been a close and intimate one, the loss of companion, lover and friend as the sufferer's ability to communicate deteriorates can lead to an increase in feelings of depression (Morris *et al.*, 1988).

The closeness and extent of support among the wider network of family and friends is also important. The majority of elderly people with families do receive support from their family if it is needed. However, according to Wenger (1987), there seem to be different types of support networks, ranging from those with local family, friends and neighbours, where an elderly person has been a long-established resident of a particular community, to networks with mainly friends and neighbours and distant kin, to those who are relatively isolated, with no local friends and no nearby family. Wenger (1987) actually discusses five different network types which offer different types and levels of support. For instance, friends are perhaps more important for good morale than family. Sadly, for both the dementia sufferer and the carer, being able to maintain friendships is limited when forgetfulness and communication problems develop.

Families living close by are able to provide more practical support than those who have moved away. In areas with a highly mobile population there is likely to be a greater need for statutory home care services than where there is population stability. Towns on the south coast of England have a population of elderly people who have moved away from family, friends and neighbours. In areas like this the burden on a spouse caring for a dementia sufferer will be especially great and there may be a need for home care, day care and other support, perhaps earlier in the illness than might be expected in areas where there are close geographical links with friends, family and neighbours which have been long established. Flexible services for dementia sufferers and their carers would take into account the nature of social and family networks and be able to work along with them.

Coping with Caring at Home

Carers have different ways of coping with caring. For some it seems that information gathering, making use of services such as day care, home help and mobile meals and drawing on family support help most. For others, 'psychological' strategies are important. These include finding an explanation for the illness and seeing positive sides to the situation. One carer commented, "In the early stages we were able to talk about things, all the good times we'd had as well as the problems. It reinforced our love for one another. I don't think we'd have done that if it hadn't been for his illness."

Denial that there is an illness is a strategy used by some carers. In such cases problems such as forgetfulness are attributed to 'old age' and sometimes specialist services will be refused. Ignoring the dementing relative and withdrawing from caring can also occur. It is important that those working with families recognise that there will be differences in people's coping strategies and work with them accordingly. For instance, to suggest attendance at relative support groups or providing information on RO and memory aids to carers who believe there is no particular illness present may be to confront them with a reality they are unable to deal with at that time.

A study by Mary Gilhooly (1984) which looked in detail at the differences between carers' ways of coping found that more men than women used practical strategies, such as making use of services on offer. Women, on the other hand, were more likely to use the psychological strategies. It is important for professionals to recognise that at times there is not a conscious choice of coping strategy made. A study of users of domiciliary support revealed that male carers were more likely to be provided with this sort of support than female carers and it may be that assumptions are made about women's abilities to provide meals, wash and dress the dementia sufferer, without a detailed examination of their coping strategies being carried out. An assessment which looks at real needs of carers can help establish whether doing household chores or sitting with a sufferer to let a carer go out for an afternoon might be the best way of helping them cope.

Physical Dependence

Physical dependency is better tolerated by families than the challenge and strain of disruptive behaviour. This may be owing to the fact that task-centred activities are easier for the carer to cope with emotionally. Providing total nursing care for a bed-bound individual may be easier to deal with than the worry and strain of caring for someone who wanders away from home and regularly gets lost in the streets nearby.

Abuse

The strain on carers, both physical and emotional, can put both carer and dependant at risk. Physical and emotional abuse of older people by carers is an under-researched area. One survey estimated that 500,000 elderly people are at risk of abuse from carers. Sexual abuse is not unknown. In some cases spouses will feel aware that they may be exploiting and taking advantage of a partner who is unable to say 'no'.

How then can professionals working with dementia sufferers and their families help to meet their needs? Flexibility of approach is vital. There is a need for intervention at the right point in the dementia process. Too early and the family will see no need for help, and may not receive it when they need it because they have refused contact with the caring agencies, too late and crisis may have occurred and appropriate management may be difficult to co-ordinate. GPs, social workers and community nurses need to let carers know they are available on the end of a telephone line if needed in the future and not be content to 'let people get on with it' if they say they are managing.

Guilty feelings about being an inadequate carer may mean that carers are reluctant to ask for help when they need it. In many cases carers need help and encouragement to relinquish the total responsibility for caring. Sensitivity on behalf of social workers, nursing staff, doctors and other professionals working with families is vital here.

Sometimes family therapy involving several family members (this may or may not include the dementia sufferer, depending on their degree of impairment) can be helpful, particularly if some members of a family are feeling aggrieved or unhappy about the way other members are dealing with the dementia. Therapy can be a forum for a more objective look at feelings, a sharing of ideas and work towards overcoming a problem. People sometimes think they understand everyone else in the family and jump to unhelpful conclusions, as in the following example.

Case example

> Mrs Kay, aged 80, was a widow with two daughters: Stella was single and lived with her mother; May was married, had one son and lived 30 miles away. Stella was angry because she felt that May was leaving her to do all the caring for her mother. She resented the fact that May had only once offered to take her mother for a visit in the last 18 months. May, on the other hand, felt that Stella was better than she was at handling her mother's difficult behaviour. She felt inadequate and had not asked her mother to stay as she felt Stella would look down on the offer and consider the care she would provide inadequate. The daughters were able to show their feelings for the first time in a family therapy session with a clinical psychologist and began to understand one another's feelings and how they had arrived at these conclusions. Soon a plan was made whereby May and her family would visit for the weekend and stay at Stella and Mrs Kay's home. Stella then went out on the Saturday evening and Sunday afternoon.

Families and Residential Care

Families often experience tremendous guilt over the issue of admitting a loved one to residential or hospital care and may feel embarrassed and harshly judged by others, as revealed by such comments as: "I felt that I had let her down. We'd always been so close. But I've had two heart attacks and some days I can barely get myself, let alone my wife, out of bed."; "I just feel that my father provided for us when we were children. He's had a hard life and I feel we owe it to him to look after him."

The cause of infrequent visiting may be that relatives experience grief and guilt on these occasions and feel unable to disclose this. Professionals need to be aware of this and provide time for the relative to voice such feelings, particularly when arrangements for residential care are being made. Staff in hospital and residential homes can encourage relatives to continue to be involved at a level they feel comfortable with.

Thus it is not only important to provide carers with the emotional support they need while they are looking after a relative at home; it is also vital to help them with the transition between home and residential or hospital care and to maintain the link with them as 'family carers' once an individual has been admitted to care. Not everyone wishes to relinquish their caring role when a relative has been admitted to hospital or residential care, but sometimes they may feel that they have to.

Is there a need for permanent long-stay care?

As it seems that carers are sometimes more able to deal with physical dependency than with wandering or demands for attention it may be that greater flexibility in the provision of care for dementia sufferers is necessary. Thus, instead of a person being admitted to residential care permanently, they could be admitted and cared for at the times when the emotional burden is likely to be greatest on carers. This may be in the early and middle stages of the illness, for instance when the person is still mobile and active and requiring a great deal of attention and support throughout the day. There should be the option that they can return home with appropriate domiciliary and community nursing support if the family feel they would like to provide care at home from time to time. This may be more likely towards the terminal stage of the disease when the person is more restricted in their activities, and is chair- or bed-bound. This fits with other care-giving models such as in the case of cancer sufferers.

Similarly, while partners or children identify the need for permanent care because they can no longer cope with intensive caring, they are often keen to have the sufferer home for a day or weekend. However the generation of people over the age of 65, who include many of the main carers of dementia sufferers, can feel nervous of what they see as authority: "I don't like to ask if she can come home on a Sunday for the day in case it's too much trouble for them to get her ready. I suppose I'm also scared that they'll think that if I can cope on a Sunday I can cope full-time."

Meeting the Needs of Carers

Services available to help dementia sufferers and their carers vary from area to area. What suits one sufferer and their family may not be helpful for another. However the following have been found to be of help by different individuals.

Carers' support groups

These exist to provide information and advice to carers, as well as allowing them to share their experiences of the burden of care and to support one another in coping with caring. As mentioned earlier, some carers find factual information most helpful while others may prefer sharing their experiences and hearing those of others. Carer's groups can usefully incorporate both of these types of support. A programme of guest speakers (eg. social worker, nurse, psychogeriatrician, chiropodist, solicitor, OT, psychologist) can be invited to talk on matters of interest to relatives, such as arranging day and respite care, medication, the latest research on dementia, foot care, looking after the financial affairs of a dementia sufferer, mobility problems, managing memory problems and dealing with wandering. The first hour or so of a two-hour meeting can be devoted to the topic introduced by the speakers; during the second hour tea and biscuits can be served and carers encouraged to talk about how things have been since the last meeting. Since family carers expend a great deal of energy on looking after their loved ones, groups are most likely to be successful if the responsibility for inviting speakers, arranging the venue and providing tea is assumed by a professional as part of their job. Regular (twice monthly) meetings with offers of transport and the availability of another room where someone can sit with any sufferers who could not be left at home will enhance the usefulness of carers' support groups.

The need for relative support groups does not stop once the sufferer is admitted to residential care. As we have seen, there remains a need for some carers to have access to a forum where they can continue to share their feelings and concerns with others.

Respite care

Attendance at day centres for dementia sufferers and regular one- or two-week stays in a hospital, local authority or private home are often suggested to or requested by the carers of dementia sufferers. However the needs of the sufferer need to be taken into account too. What will be the effect of time spent away from home? In some cases disorientation and confusion may be increased after a one- or two-week stay away, with a consequent increase in demands on the carer. Where day care is concerned, although a break for the carer may be crucial, the type of stimulation offered to the dementia sufferer at the day centre must be considered. Some day care provision merely provides meals and ensures the basic safety of the sufferer (ie checking that they do not wander away) but offers no therapeutic activity which may be of positive benefit. Often the levels of staff needed to care and provide therapeutic activity for dementia sufferers are too low.

Weekend and night respite (particularly for those caring for sufferers who are alert and wakeful at night) may be of more value to some carers than weekday day care. Likewise the opportunity to use a hospital bed for a dementia sufferer one week in six instead of permanently may be preferred. Discussions with carers' groups may help planners of services to meet local needs, rather than expecting individuals to fit into services.

Domiciliary support

As has already been mentioned, the needs of the dementia sufferer have to be considered alongside those of the carers. Some dementia sufferers have been lifelong loners or simply prefer to stay at home. Care in the home may therefore be the preferred option. Many carers reject the offer of home care or sitting services because they claim that they do not need help with housework.

However home help and home care services are now geared more to helping the dementia sufferer with dressing or bathing and simple domestic routines, so that the main carer can have a break either in or out of the home. Sitting services are sometimes provided by statutory or voluntary agencies and can provide people who will sit with a sufferer who cannot be left alone, while carers go out to shop or visit friends.

Advice, counselling and therapy

Easy access via GP or self-referral to professionals experienced in dealing with dementia sufferers is important. Carers should have a named individual and phone number to call if they wish to. Sometimes carers' support groups arrange telephone links between new and old members. Counselling and therapy such as the family therapy already mentioned may also be provided in some areas.

Conclusion

To summarise, it should be possible for a package of care to be arranged which makes use of available services and takes the needs of both sufferer and carers into account. Flexible care arrangements, continued counselling and involvement with other carers should also be available for families who have a relative in permanent residential or hospital care. Professionals need to be aware of all the services available in a particular area and who to contact to discuss providing them. Integration of services and flexibility are crucial to helping carers to cope.

REFERENCES

Gilhooly M, 'The impact of caregiving on caregivers: factors associated with the psychological well-being of people supporting a dementing relative in the community', *British Journal of Medical Psychology* 57, pp 35–44, 1984.

Gilleard C J, *Living with Dementia: Community Care of the Elderly Mentally Infirm*, Croom Helm, 1984.

Morris L W, Morris R G and Britton, P G, 'The relationship between marital intimacy, perceived strain and depression in spouse caregivers of dementia sufferers', *British Journal of Medical Psychology* 61, pp 231–6, 1988.

Wenger G C, *Relationships in Old Age — inside support networks: third report of a follow-up study of old people in North Wales,* Report to DHSS/Welsh Office, Centre for Social Policy, Research and Development, University College of North Wales, Bangor, 1987.

FURTHER READING

Herr J J and Weakland J H, *Counselling Elders and their Families,* Springer, New York, 1979.

Wenger G C and Shahtahmasebi S, *Variations in Support Networks: some social policy implications,* Centre for Social Policy, Research and Development, University College of North Wales, Bangor, 1988.

Woods R T, *Alzheimer's Disease: Coping with a Living Death,* Souvenir Press, 1989.

Coping with Professional Caring

When pursuing excellence in client care, consideration for the health and well-being of those delivering the service is essential. Being responsible and accountable for the care dementing people receive can be rewarding, yet it may also prove to be excessively demanding, both emotionally and physically. This may be stimulating in the short term, but, if the demands are unremitting, the work can become a powerful source of stress and strain for the care-provider.

Stress

Lazarus and Folkman (1984) defined stress as reflecting a relationship or transaction between the person and the environment which taxes or exceeds their adjustive resources. The result is an unpleasant internal state of excessive anxiety and negative emotion. Each person will find different situations or events stressful, according to their own adaptive resources. Thus, except in the most extreme circumstances, it is not possible to predict in advance those demands which have the potential to stress. The experience of stress is unique to each individual.

The stress of working with dementia sufferers

Attempting to meet the needs of dementing people who are destined to deteriorate can be disheartening. Although appropriate goal setting and sensitive therapeutic practice can lead to encouraging levels of client improvement, other characteristics of the work can be debilitating. The work is often physically hard, the hours can be both long and unsocial, and respect for 'the job done' often difficult to detect. In residential homes and on hospital wards staffing levels are invariably poor, and this may reflect the low priority and corresponding low status attached to working with dementia sufferers. Community workers can become disheartened with inadequate domiciliary and respite resources, and exasperated by the difficulties experienced in gaining access to such services.

The expectations of others, especially senior management and, on occasions, relatives, may be unrealistic. With limited resources staff are expected to provide not only a safe system of care but one which satisfies standards of quality. The difficulties are compounded when decisions affecting the organisation of service delivery are outside the control of those providing the care. Feelings of helplessness and uncertainty magnify the unpleasant experience of stress.

Tension within a staff group may arise for many reasons. The delivery of quality care is largely based on team work. However, if members of the group are not working towards a common goal, then frustrations and disagreements can easily develop. When a staff group undergoes changes new members may be unclear as to their responsibilities and experience 'role uncertainty'. When staff have differing expectations of each other 'role conflict' can arise. This can be a powerful source of group tension and stress as a person finds their ability to work is undermined by the conflict between their interpretation of role obligations and the differing expectations of others.

Unrealistic self-expectations can also induce a state of stress. Believing that you can master all situations that arise, and that you must get on well with, and meet the needs of, all clients is evidence of dysfunctional expectations. It would seem that nurses have high expectations of themselves, and as a profession are not supportive of each other.

Burn-out

When a carer is subject to sustained and excessive levels of stress the outcome can be *burn-out*. This condition was first described by Freudenberger (1975) in terms of 'physical and emotional exhaustion including the development of negative self-concepts, negative job attitudes and a loss of concern and feelings for clients'.

A stressed carer may become irritable and be easily angered by trivial events. They may lack patience with both colleagues and dependants, and present as critical, moody and resentful. Burn-out may also result in indifference towards their work and colleagues. Staff may withdraw from client contact, typically retreating to the office to do 'paperwork' or finding sanctuary in 'household' tasks such as making beds or tidying a room. Thus task-oriented care may, in part, be a dysfunctional coping strategy for staff faced with the unremitting and unpredictable demands of communicating with and caring for seriously confused people. Table 24.1 identifies these and other major signs of burn-out.

Table 24.1
Burn-out: signs and symptoms

■Persistent resistance to going to work
■Fatigue
■'Clockwatching'
■Indifference
■Negative work attitudes
■Isolation
■Resistance to direct client contact
■Cynicism
■Feeling discouraged
■Sense of failure and guilt
■Rigidity in modes of thinking and practice
■Absenteeism because of sickness. Common physical symptoms:
     Exhaustion
     Gastro-intestinal problems; for example, nausea, vomiting and
          diarrhoea
     Backache
     Loss of appetite
     Weight loss
     Headache
     Insomnia

Eventually the burned-out staff member can lower morale generally and the care team as a whole may struggle to function.

Managing Stress

Mutual support

As a regular practice promote the mutual support of colleagues through a recognised staff-support network. Hold staff meetings to exchange experiences and concerns. Do not feel embarrassed to acknowledge your doubts and weaknesses, for you will also undoubtedly have assets and strengths from which your fellow carers may benefit. The group should be closed, and members should be encouraged to express negative feelings, disappointments and aspirations without fear of condemnation. An outside facilitator may be of value to the group if help is needed to direct discussions and there is need for impartial interpretations of contentious issues. Overall, staff must have confidence in the confidential and non-judgemental procedures of the meetings.

Psychological strategies

Where you see weakness and ineffectiveness in yourself, are your judgements overly harsh and out of line with reality? Are you distorting your view of events by imposing unrealistic personal standards? To one person 91 per cent in an examination is an outstanding success, to another it is a failure. Same event, different expectations. Always check whether your worries are unfounded or exaggerated.

Try to develop coping attitudes. Dismiss negative and self-defeating ideas. Do not let your mind run riot to an extent that you feel overwhelmed by your responsibilities. Abandon 'what if . . .' thoughts. Be constructive and concentrate on the task at hand. The demands and pressures may appear endless but you will only get on top of them if you tackle one problem at a time. Positive thinking can help prevent undesirable levels of stress and strain.

Reduce the pressure you feel by avoiding such ideas as 'I *should* be doing better' or 'I *must* do that.' Such pressure thoughts increase the demands you place on yourself and make caring even more tiring. The strain can be bad enough to handle without inflicting more and more pressure upon yourself. You may *prefer* to be more able, or you may *like* to be more successful, but nowhere is it written that you *should* be more able or that you *must* be successful. The 'tyranny of the should' only serves to generate strain and undermine performance.

If you are struggling and finding work exhausting, try to place your weaknesses and shortcomings in perspective. Set them alongside areas of performance which are not suffering. It is easy to focus on our failures, ignore our strengths and then regard ourselves as totally inadequate. By introducing balance into self-evaluation, you are likely to be more productive, as you will no longer be plagued and distracted by self-doubt.

All in all, adopting the right attitudes can make you a more effective care-giver and, as a result, can help those people you are caring for obtain a better quality of life.

Emotional distance

If you never distance yourself from your work, burn-out is more likely to occur. Distancing is not just a matter of putting physical distance between yourself and the workplace, but also means 'switching off' and freeing yourself from work concerns. We all need a break from demanding responsibilities, so to be an effective carer you need to 'recharge the batteries', not only through rest and relaxation, but also by gaining involvement and satisfaction from life away from work.

At work the emotional needs of staff need to be acknowledged. The opportunity to take breaks away from the needs of clients is essential, otherwise fatigue and intolerance characterise relationships, and care-givers will develop their own methods of escape by seeking sanctuary in non-essential 'hotel' or office tasks.

Time management

Prioritising tasks and obligations may serve to reduce the pressure of work and lead to time being used more effectively. Learning to say 'no' when already burdened by duties, without feeling guilty or disloyal, can be a critical step towards avoiding an accumulation of stress. Taking time out to plan the activities of the following day and to evaluate existing routines may identify practices which undermine staff performance and cause avoidable strain. Limitations imposed on care-providers by organisational demands are a major source of burn-out. It is unrealistic to view work stress as being an individual difficulty divorced from the organisation of work. Resolution of the former may often require the restructuring of the latter.

Conclusion

It is widely recognised that caring is a stressful profession. However, much can be done by staff to reduce the prospect of burn-out by maximising 'adjustive resources' and reviewing organisational demands. The acknowledgement that caring environments for elderly confused people are stressful means that senior management also need to appreciate that, to avoid high rates of staff burn-out, sensitive and effective support structures are essential. Furthermore morale and thus work performance can be markedly improved by management recognising that working with dementing people is a skilled area of care practice which cannot be performed by ill-informed, over-burdened staff.

If the needs of staff are neglected we run the risk of sacrificing any professed intention to be working for the well-being of dementing people dependent on professional care-givers for their physical and emotional welfare.

REFERENCES

Freudenberger H J, 'The staff burn-out syndrome in alternative institutions', *Psychotherapy: Theory research and practice* 12, pp 73–82, 1975.
Lazarus R S and Folkman S, *Stress, Appraisal, and Coping*, Springer, New York, 1984.

FURTHER READING

Bailey R D, *Coping with Stress in Caring*, Blackwell Scientific Publications, Oxford, 1985.
Hodgkinson P, 'Nursing stress', *Nursing Times* p 33, 10 Oct. 1984.

OTHER USEFUL BOOKS FROM WINSLOW

*Winslow Press publishes a wide range of materials specifically for those caring for and working with the elderly. Listed below are just a few of these titles – a full catalogue is available **free** on request.*

Managing Common Problems with the Elderly Confused

Graham Stokes

Of vital importance to every carer, these four books offer positive and practical advice on problem behaviours that commonly occur amongst elderly confused people. *Wandering, Screaming and Shouting, Incontinence and Inappropriate Urinating* and *Aggression* make up the series.

Looking at Confusion

Una Holden

A controversial topic which is tackled in a practical and straightforward way. This book will help you devise ideas for training programmes, establish a useful working concept of dementia and find a logical way to look at, and begin to understand, the many facets of dementia.

Reminiscence with Elderly People

Andrew Norris

A very practical paperback which enables you to maximise the benefits of this therapeutic method. All aspects of reminiscence therapy are covered in clear and simple language.

Groupwork and the Elderly

Mike Bender, Andrew Norris & Paulette Bauckham

Here is a practical manual for staff who wish to establish or improve groupwork within any day care or residential setting. Topics covered include: attitudes to ageing; the nature and purpose of groups and the practicalities of running groups for confused elderly people.

Counselling Carers

Andrew Papadopoulos

A practical guide for those who would like to acquire or develop the skills necessary for supporting and counselling the relatives and friends who care for confused elderly people. Advice on setting up a client-centred relative support service is included.

The Reminiscence Puzzle Book

Robert Dynes

Spanning the years 1930-1989, this is a highly practical and enjoyable puzzle book covering events, people, entertainment and everyday life in the past. It will encourage group participants to recall their own personal experiences.

Groupwork Activities

Danny Walsh

Groupwork Activities is a huge collection of tried and tested practical activities and ideas which can be used with every group of older people. Illustrating how groupwork can be both fun and therapeutic, this book contains a host of well presented ideas for word puzzles, quizzes, outdoor pursuits, relaxation, art, music, crafts, memory games, reminiscence, RO, domestic tasks and day trips.

Develop an Activities Programme

Theresa Briscoe

All you need to know about setting up an activities programme for elderly people is to be found in this original and informative manual. The text contains ideas that have been thoroughly field tested by the author who has gained recognition as 'Nurse of the Year' for her work in this field. Also included are helpful photocopiable programmes and ideas, such as job descriptions, equipment, surveys and plans.

For further information, please contact us at the adjacent address

WINSLOW

Telford Road • Bicester
Oxon OX6 0TS • UK
Tel: 01869 244644
Fax: 01869 320040